2.00

"They say that experience is the be
have experienced what they write at
Aaron Früh has delivered life-transforming truths birthed out of overcoming the trials he has encountered. Because of this he is a voice I trust. Practical, insightful, and applicable, the principles he shares will renew your mind-set and transform your life."

Michelle McKinney Hammond,
author of *Get Over It and On with It*

"In *Bounce*, Aaron Früh gives you a clear strategy for coming back from defeat. If you are in the valley of disappointment, this book is a must-read. Aaron will help you discover that returning to the land of the living is not as long of a journey as you might think."

Crane Durham, president and host of Nothing but Truth,
a nationally syndicated radio program
on American Family Radio Network

"Aaron Früh shines a bright light of truth on the crippling effects of loss and discouragement. His insight reminded me of one of my favorite songs that says 'A saint is just a sinner who fell down and got up.'"

Jackie Patillo, president and executive director
of The Gospel Music Association

"This book will help you bounce back from the pain of loss and disappointment. It is full of hope and encouragement, and Aaron will help you navigate through your challenges so you can make a real comeback. If you have experienced pain, loss, and disappointment, then this book is a must-read."

Michael Coleman, president and CEO of Israel Team;
cofounder and former CEO of Integrity Media

"Who among us doesn't need encouragement? In his most recent book, *Bounce*, Aaron Früh takes us through the steps of how God's

Word provides the road map in overcoming and thriving during adversity. Aaron shares that the daunting task of facing loss can be turned into an opportunity to create life-changing resiliency and equip us with tools to handle the changing seasons of our lives."

Stuart J. Roth practices constitutional and international law in Washington, DC

"There are nearly eight billion people on earth, and all of us will face some form of adversity. All experiences will do something for you or something to you. I have learned that every setback can make you bitter or better, and it is your choice. Adversity will only visit the strong but will stay forever with the weak. In this book, Aaron Früh challenges you to meet adversity head-on and press on regardless of your heartaches and losses. I believe that if you always try to do your best and never give up, eventually God will take care of everything else."

Coach Dale Brown, LSU basketball coach 1972–1997; college basketball hall of fame member

"Very few people want to discuss loss, and fewer still are able discuss it in a productive, purposeful way—but that is exactly what Aaron Früh has done in this book. *Bounce* is a remarkably pleasant read, skillfully weaving together historical accounts, personal anecdotes, solid theological understanding, and pragmatic wisdom. But more importantly, *Bounce* is a valuable field guide that equips readers to grow through, not merely get through, experiences that are remarkably unpleasant."

Thomas Arington, chairman of Prasco Laboratories, Cincinnati, Ohio

Patty,
Press On Regardless!

BOUNCE

Learning to
THRIVE
through Loss, Tragedy,
and Heartache

AARON FRÜH

BakerBooks
a division of Baker Publishing Group
Grand Rapids, Michigan

© 2017 by Aaron Früh

Published by Baker Books
a division of Baker Publishing Group
P.O. Box 6287, Grand Rapids, MI 49516-6287
www.bakerbooks.com

Printed in the United States of America

Library of Congress Cataloging-in-Publication Data is on file at the Library of Congress, Washington, DC.

978-0-8010-7515-5

The author is represented by the literary agency of William K. Jensen Literary Agency.

17 18 19 20 21 22 23   7 6 5 4 3 2 1

For Nora

Nobody ever lives their life all the way up except bull-fighters.

Ernest Hemingway, *The Sun Also Rises*

CONTENTS

PART 1

The Keys to Resilience Are within You

1

Matthew Lawson's Paper Plates

Strength is not created by adversity; it is merely awakened by it.

Mark Eddy Smith, *Tolkien's Ordinary Virtues: Exploring the Spiritual Themes of the Lord of the Rings*

Matthew Lawson lived and died without much fanfare. The only proof I have of his existence is a worn-out photograph from the 1960s and a story. The photo is of Matthew, standing in front of his desk piled high with history books and wearing an Indiana Jones–style hat, leather jacket, and a holster around his waist, with a six-shooter in hand and a sly half smile simmering on his lips. An old oil portrait of an Apache Indian chief hangs on the wall behind him. The colors of Matthew Lawson's photograph all seem to have merged with age. Polaroid, perhaps? It's not such a great picture, but the story, well, that's something else. When I heard it, it stopped me in my tracks.

Matthew Lawson's life can be summed up by one thing he did every summer, year after year, without fail. Imagine your life story being framed by one action that left such a deep impression on others they would repeat it often, with enthusiasm. This one unique thing still has people talking and reminiscing about him—and still trying to figure out why he did it.

Matthew Lawson's story plays out in the wildlands of Mexico, where he went to live each summer. Every July he compelled his wife and three children to leave their comfortable home in Arizona and trek across the border to join him. Friends also joined the family from as far away as Ohio. Every summer, year after year, they followed Matthew Lawson into the wilderness.

To find the perfect camp for the large entourage, Matthew Lawson would cross the border early and alone. Family and friends knew the region where Matthew prepared their shelter but never the exact location.

With no cell phone to communicate his whereabouts, Matthew Lawson would drive stakes along the dirt roads and attach white paper plates as directional signs. As the sojourners got closer to their destination, so did the space between the plates. The story is fascinating because of the three letters Matthew Lawson wrote on each plate. Those three letters written on cheap paper plates represent three of the most inspiring words ever penned, words that challenged their readers to commit themselves to resilience no matter their circumstances. These three letters inspired his family and friends to keep forging down the trail despite any fear of wild beasts or getting lost. As long as they saw the three letters, they knew they were going to make it through the wilderness and eventually find Matthew Lawson.

The Wisdom in Three Simple Letters

The simple letters on those paper plates would impact the lives of Matthew Lawson's three children so deeply that they would become models of resilience, rebounding through those wilderness

12

seasons when all they had was a dusty road and three letters to hold on to. His children taught the meaning of those three letters to their children, and they also taught it to me.

I never met Matthew Lawson. He passed away twenty-five years ago. I am sure greater stories have been told about resilience but I was captivated by his story and the three letters that anchor it. What would drive a man to draw his family into unknown wilderness? What kind of a man takes the time to write three letters on twenty or thirty paper plates, attach them to wooden stakes, and then hammer the stakes alongside some dusty back roads? Either Matthew Lawson was a wild-eyed, crazed adventurer or he was doing the one thing, if done regularly and often enough, that would cause his children to understand an important life principle. In the end, it would be the greatest thing they would remember about him.

And what are the three letters? POR. These three letters represent words so powerful that if you will follow their encouraging, even commanding, declaration, you, too, will become a model of resilience, never being held back by discouragement, loss, or circumstances no matter how difficult your wilderness experience.

The three words are *Press On Regardless*. With POR, Matthew Lawson taught his kids to keep moving through the wilderness and refuse to get stuck there by pressing on regardless of fear, difficulty, or fatigue. A wise man once said, "If you're going through hell, keep going." Matthew Lawson taught his children one of the most profound lessons of life: how to remain resilient in the face of struggle or pain. *Resilience* is the time-tested truth that we can all bounce back better and stronger after a traumatic loss—if we will just keep pressing on regardless.

In our world today, this truth needs to be examined and investigated once again. It's worrisome that we have become a generation who has lost the raw nerve to keep going when we've hit bottom.

That's why I love Matthew Lawson's story! This story first unfolded to me when I overheard his daughter say, "POR!" when she was facing a tough life challenge. "POR?" I inquired. "Press on regardless!" she shot back.

I have no idea where Matthew Lawson first heard the words *press on regardless*. Because he loved history—military history, to be exact—some say he borrowed the phrase from the Royal British Air Force (RAF). The famous Battle of Britain was fought in the air, and the Brits were severely outnumbered by the Nazi Luftwaffe. Those three encouraging words, *press on regardless*, were used by British commanders to inspire pilots and crews to guide their planes through enemy fire, poor weather conditions, and miles of territory often traveled with low fuel reserves.

So maybe Matthew Lawson borrowed the phrase from British military history. Or maybe he just made it up himself. I don't know how he came to use these three standout words, but he certainly created a one-of-a-kind story around them. Where will POR lead us? Let's find out.

Our Path toward Resilience

In this book we are going to investigate how we can rebound from the traumas of life and bounce back stronger, happier, and wiser than before. The truth Matthew Lawson taught his children with a black marker and paper plates in the barren landscape of the desert can be your truth as well. You too can learn the exhilarating wonder of character that allows you to be knocked down at times but come back stronger than ever.

Sadly, many never quite make it through suffering the shock of loss. They are stuck somewhere in the middle of a parentheses. The emotional devastation loss brings is a game changer. Loss has stolen initiative from myriads of souls: rich, poor, big, small, great intellects, and simpletons. Loss is no respecter of persons. Most likely you picked up this book or someone gave it to you because you have suffered a setback.

Like many others, you may have experienced a financial loss in these days of worldwide economic uncertainty. Perhaps you've lost a business or retirement portfolio. Maybe you've confronted a setback in your career and now you're working two jobs. You may even have joined the unemployment lines. Or, with all of the outside pressure on families, your marriage may have suffered a breakup and you're mourning the disintegration of your home. Perhaps you've lost a loved one through sickness, tragic accident, or suicide.

In all honesty, you may be thinking you're not able to rebound this time. Game over. You may be reading these pages and are already thinking of checking out. I encourage you to finish this book before you sell your business, leave your marriage, quit the ministry, or make a rash decision because you are clouded by the pain of the moment. One of my favorite lines from the Bible is, "And it came to pass."

■ ■ ■

This book is organized into three parts. In part 1, you will discover that you have been wonderfully designed for resilience, you will learn how to reframe your perspective of loss, and you will discover three powerful questions whose honest answers will inspire you to begin the journey back to the land of the living. In part 2 you will look at four resilience blockers and how to defeat them. Be prepared for intense work, honesty, and transparency in this section, because fortified obstacles to resilience don't budge easily. Highlighting part 3 are four ways to activate your comeback.

And, by the way, you are coming back, I promise you. I can make this promise because the core principle of this book—that you can bounce back from life's painful losses—is actually a deeply rooted idea that comes straight from God's heart to us through

His Word, the Bible. We will discover the far-reaching significance of the biblical call to a resilient life throughout this book, but first let's consider two statements from the apostle Paul:

> Not that I am saying this to call attention to any need of mine; since, as far as I am concerned, I have learned to be content *regardless of circumstances*. I know what it is to be in want, and I know what it is to have more than enough—in everything and in every way I have learned the secret of being full and being hungry, of having abundance and being in need. (Phil. 4:11–12 CJB, emphasis added)

> Brothers and sisters, I do not consider myself yet to have taken hold of it. But one thing I do: Forgetting what is behind and straining toward what is ahead, I *press on* toward the goal to win the prize for which God has called me heavenward in Christ Jesus. (3:13–14 NIV, emphasis added)

In the first passage, Paul lets us in on his secret of dealing with the reality of loss: he has learned to be content regardless of circumstances. This is a penetrating statement. It tells me the brash tenacity it takes to press on regardless is not something you are born with but rather something you learn. Pressing on regardless of circumstances had nothing to do with Paul's personality but was a part of his character, learned over time through his relationship with Christ. This is great news because the belief that people are resilient by nature is simply not true. We will uncover this fallacy in our next chapter and discover the encouraging reality that the rebounding spirit is available for everyone!

In the second passage, Paul tells us he disregards the failures and mistakes of his past, forgetting what is behind and pressing on. He is saying, "Whatever happened to you yesterday, whatever loss you endured, press on regardless." The word translated "press" in Greek is *dioko*, and it means "to pursue by speeding on earnestly." The word translated "goal" or "mark" in Greek is *skopos*. Paul is using athletic terms from the Olympic games. As the runners raced they "pressed on" by speeding earnestly toward the *skopos*, the rectangular pillar at the far end of the Roman coliseum. They focused their eyes on the *skopos* rather than turning their heads and looking behind in order to see if they were winning or losing. The runners were trained to focus on the *skopos* and press on regardless of their status in the race. Paul's *skopos* was God's call upon his life, his personal destiny.

My prayer for you is that by the end of this book you will learn Paul's secret of bouncing back from life's perils and pitfalls and focus your eyes once again on the *skopos*, reaching your personal God-ordained destiny. Paul learned how to press on regardless, and so can you! So, if you will permit me to be your Matthew Lawson, I have a black marker, a stack of paper plates, some wooden stakes, and a hammer. I would be honored to lead you across the border. Will you take this journey with me and learn the joys of bouncing back?

In our next chapter, I'm going to introduce you to a children's storybook character you may have more in common with than you think.

POR!

BOUNCE TAKEAWAY:
Reflect on Your Own Story

1. Who is the most resilient person you have ever met?
2. What lesson did this person teach you about resilience?
3. Are issues from your past (a failure that has opened the door to shame, a tragedy, a loss, a heartache that has left you clawing for answers) keeping you from pressing on regardless? What are these issues?

As we begin this study on resilience I encourage you to purchase a journaling book. On the cover write: "My Bounce Journal." Your first challenge begins with writing these words on the first page of your bounce journal: "Bounce Challenge #1" (there will be twelve bounce challenges, so you can write this headline for each challenge and number them accordingly).

BOUNCE CHALLENGE #1

I will press on regardless of . . . List all of the things that come to your mind that are keeping you from bouncing back.

2

You Were Made to Bounce

> The human capacity for burden is like bamboo—far
> more flexible than you'd ever believe at first glance.
>
> Jodi Picoult, *My Sister's Keeper*

If you ask my twenty-two-year-old daughter Hannah who her favorite literary character is, it's Tigger, hands down, that lovable, orange-and-black-striped furry tiger originally appearing in A. A. Milne's book *The House at Pooh Corner*. Of all the creatures in Pooh's Hundred Acre Wood, Tigger is known for his remarkable resilience. As Tigger sings in the classic Walt Disney movie of the book, he's got a top made of rubber and a bottom made of springs. Tigger joyfully ends his song with the words, "But the most wonderful thing about Tiggers is I'm the only one."[1] There is only one Tigger, this unique bouncy, pouncy creature with a top made out of rubber and a bottom made out of springs.

We admire people who, like Tigger, seem to have the capacity to bounce back from their troubles. We long for their resilient qualities. Our favorite human interest stories are of people who have suffered the loss of everything only to come back stronger. We watch these Tiggers from a distance, believing that they're unique, special, and anomalous freaks of nature. They are built to bounce right through the pain and tragedy of their losses, only to complete the journey unscathed and remarkably happier than ever before. They bounce back from failure with effortless wonder. We think that somehow God must have given them extraordinary padding—a top made out of rubber and a bottom made out of springs. We honestly believe that the most wonderful thing about Tiggers is that they're the only ones. But the fact is, like Tigger, you were made to bounce.

The word *resilience* has been with us a long time and is of Latin and Old English origins. In short, it simply means "to bounce back." And by our very nature, that's what we are: resilient.

Created to Withstand Pressure and Heal

Consider your spinal column. The spine is made up of thirty-three bony pieces called vertebrae. These bones are stabilized by ligaments and separated by twenty-three intervertebral shock absorbers called disks. You have six disks in your neck, twelve in the middle of your back, and five in your lower back. This amazing design allows you to absorb the crushing blows your body experiences when running, jumping, or simply walking across a room. Without these shock absorbers, your back bones would slowly be crushed by pressure in the most common ritual of getting out of bed in the morning, let alone running a marathon or jumping in a gunny sack race on the Fourth of July. You were made to bounce. You were created with physical qualities that allow you to absorb the impact of shock and pressure without being crushed.

Your body also has the ability to heal itself. If you cut your hand, the wound will automatically begin to repair. This resilient healing process is constantly in motion in your body. It's what helps you rebound from wear and tear. Dying cells are replaced with new ones daily. Every twenty-four hours your body produces two hundred billion new red blood cells. You feel refreshed after a good night's sleep, catch a second wind after a long day at work, and recover from a common cold or flu because your body is amazingly designed to bounce back.

We appreciate our bodies' resilience, especially when we suffer from an injury. But, for the most part, we are unaware of the awesome resilience movement going on under our skin. Have you ever wished your mind was created to be as resilient as your body? Wouldn't it be awesome if we could recover from life's crushing pressures and failures and bounce back the way our intervertebral disks do? When our life visions die, wouldn't it be comforting to know we can rejuvenate them the same way new red blood cells replace our dying ones?

The fact is, you were made to bounce back not only physically but also mentally, emotionally, and spiritually.

Think about your brain for a minute. You have one hundred billion nerve cells called neurons in your brain. These neurons explode with electrical charges three hundred billion times per second. And you wonder why you have mental fatigue after a long day at the office! These electrical charges are actually the makeup of our thoughts and words. Neurologists have discovered these electrical impulses form branches in our brains. They have found that healthy thoughts produce good trees and unhealthy thoughts produce bad trees. You could say these neuron trees are your long-term memories.

Your brain was designed by a God of love, joy, and peace. Have you ever wondered, when you have a joyful thought, why you suddenly begin to feel joyful all over? Your brain is secreting a joy chemical down your brain stem into your heart, and it's circulating through the arteries of your body. Have you ever been separated from a loved one for an extended period of time, and at the moment of reunion you are overwhelmed with the emotion of love? A love chemical has been secreted down your brain stem into your heart and then pumped through your body. Your entire nervous system is overwhelmed with love!

Have you ever felt stressed and pressured, stopped to pray, and suddenly felt peace in the midst of the storm? A peace chemical is fulfilling its God-given purpose recorded in the Scriptures: "You will keep him in perfect peace, whose mind is stayed on You, because he trusts in You" (Isa. 26:3).

Why, then, do you react physically when you are living in fear of the future? Why do you weave that proverbial knot in your stomach, find sleep difficult, and generally become irritable when you are experiencing the stress of fear? When you suffer loss and struggle with the fear of failure and doubt, how can you press on regardless of your circumstances?

A fascinating, faith-based book on the subject of the unique ability of the brain to bounce back called *Who Switched Off My Brain?* was written by Dr. Caroline Leaf, a cognitive neuroscientist. When Dr. Leaf first began practicing neurology several decades ago, the common belief within the scientific community was that the brain was not resilient. Once toxic thought patterns were formed by negative life experiences, those memory trees could not be erased. The ability to bounce back from loss was viewed as an anomaly. Dr. Leaf writes:

> The common wisdom of the time was that the brain is like a machine, and if a part is broken, it couldn't be repaired. It was believed that the brain was hardwired from birth with a fixed destiny to wear out with age. Adding this belief to the assumption that we were bound to a fate predetermined by our genes made the horizon of hope seem bleak. As you can imagine, these assumptions led to many common conclusions about the best ways to overcome the most difficult experiences, conclusions which were not based on how the brain functions. But we are no longer bound by those misperceptions. You are not a victim of biology. God has given us

a design of hope: we can switch on our brains, renew our minds, change and heal. . . .

   The implications of this are obvious: we need to take responsibility for our choices and subsequent words, actions and behavior. We can't blame anyone else.[2]

Laughter, the Best Medicine

Singer Reba McIntyre likes to repeat an old saw: "To succeed in life you need three things: a wishbone, a backbone, and a funny bone." Think back over the times in your life when you experienced a momentary discouraging setback. All seemed bleak as you counted up your losses. Bouncing back didn't seem like a viable option. Then, in the midst of this dark season, something struck you as funny. You heard a hilarious joke or watched a gut-splitting comedy, or just enjoyed a fun dinner out with really good friends where laughter was the main course of the evening. Suddenly, you felt better! For no apparent reason, your entire outlook had changed, yet your circumstances were still the same. What just happened? Dr. Leaf explains:

> Many studies show why laughter deserves to be known as "the best medicine." It releases an instant flood of feel-good chemicals that boost the immune system and almost instantly reduce levels of stress hormones. For example, a really good belly laugh can make cortisol drop by 39% and adrenalin by 70%, while the "feel-good hormone," endorphin, increases by 29%. It can even make growth hormones skyrocket by 87%! Other research shows how laughter boosts your immune system by increasing immunity levels and disease-fighting cells. . . . According to research, laughing 100 to 200 times a day is equal to 10 minutes of rowing or jogging! Laughter quite literally dissolves distressing toxic emotions because you can't feel mad or sad when you laugh: endorphins are released, making you feel so great and at peace that toxic thoughts can't get out of your brain fast enough.[3]

23

Wise King Solomon was right when he said, "A merry heart does good, like medicine, but a broken spirit dries the bones" (Prov. 17:22). Laughter is just another way the body is made to bounce.

Engineered for Pressure, with a Caveat

Later we are going to investigate God's way of renewing your mind, but let me simply say now that everything about you was designed for resilience: your bone structure, your arteries, your brain, and even your skin. You were made to bounce. You have been fearfully and wonderfully made! You were designed to bounce back stronger, happier, and wiser than before the painful wounds and traumatic blows loss left in its wake. You can press on regardless because you were designed for resilience.

The concept of resilience is even used in civil engineering to determine the ability of different kinds of material to return to their original shape after suffering pressure. Take a balloon, for example. Apply pressure with both hands to the sides of the balloon, and the weight of the pressure will change its appearance. Release the pressure and the balloon will return to its normal shape.

You came into this world under pressure. Your early prenatal health demanded it. The journey you traveled down the birth canal pressed the fluid out of your lungs, preparing them for a powerful first breath accompanied by your first ear-splitting cry! Under the extreme pressure of the birthing process, a baby's central nervous system lights up, the umbilical vessels spasm shut, a hole in the heart closes, the lungs now infiltrate and oxygenate blood, the liver metabolizes, kidneys begin to filter blood, and the gastrointestinal tract starts absorbing all nutrients. Even your skull was designed to withstand the traumatic pressure of birth.

Why have I taken the time to give such specific detail about your spinal column, your body's ability to heal itself, and your mind's complex capability to press on regardless of negative toxic thoughts and crushing pressures? I'm letting you know that a wonderful Creator has designed every human being on the face of the earth with the capacity to bounce back. It's good to know this.

However—and this is a huge however—the incredible design of our bodies is not enough to get us through the pain of loss and the tragedies of life. Our divine design serves only as a directional signpost to the loving Creator of all things, Jesus, who created us in the *Imago Dei*—the very image of God! If you don't personally know Jesus and don't have an intimate relationship with Him, you will not be able to withstand the pressures of life and endure to the end. Without Jesus on the inside, the pressure from the outside will eventually cause us to implode. This is because our bodies are designed to be a temple for God to dwell in. Take out the presence of the Holy Spirit and all you have left is an empty suit made by a great designer.

Think of the air pressure in the balloon I referred to earlier. When the inside pressure can't endure the pressure being forced upon it from the outside, it explodes. What is left is a deflated and shredded piece of synthetic material with its sides blown out. Unless you have something greater inside of you, there isn't even a slim chance you will withstand the pressures of the coming days. Self-confidence, motivation, and a positive mental attitude are not going to make the grade alone.

Let me be clear: in order to press on regardless of the pressures and losses of life, you're going to need a supernatural, holy God indwelling your spirit. The apostle Paul makes this plain:

> We are hard-pressed on every side, yet not crushed; we are per-plexed, but not in despair; persecuted, but not forsaken; struck down, but not destroyed—always carrying about in the body the dying of the Lord Jesus, that the life of Jesus also may be mani-fested in our body. For we who live are always delivered to death for Jesus' sake, that the life of Jesus also may be manifested in our

mortal flesh. . . . Therefore we do not lose heart. Even though our outward man is perishing, yet the inward man is being renewed day by day. For our light affliction, which is but for a moment, is working for us a far more exceeding and eternal weight of glory. (2 Cor. 4:8–11, 16–17)

For we do not want you to be ignorant, brethren, of our trouble which came to us in Asia: that we were burdened beyond measure, above strength, so that we despaired even of life. Yes, we had the sentence of death in ourselves, that we should not trust in ourselves but in God who raises the dead, who delivered us from so great a death, and does deliver us; in whom we trust that He will still deliver us. (1:8–10)

Paul is saying that he trusts only God, not his own abilities, and that's the only way he continues to press on. Paul understands that because the life of Jesus is inside of him, he is able to withstand the overwhelming pressures from the outside. Those same pressures are causing so many men and women today to give up on life. Actually, pressure is good. The greater your pressure, the greater your resilience. If you're not experiencing pressure, you're not growing and maturing.

Jesus Experienced Pressure

If you want to find Jesus, you will find Him in the midst of pressure. When the four friends attempted to bring their paralytic friend to Jesus for healing, they had to lower the lame man through a hole in the roof because they could not come near Him due to "the press" of the crowd (Mark 2:4 KJV). The woman with the issue of blood came to Jesus in a crowded street and touched the hem of His garment. Jesus immediately asked His disciples who had touched Him. "When all denied it, Peter and those with him said, 'Master, the multitudes throng and press You, and You say, 'Who touched Me?'" (Luke 8:45).

When Jesus prayed in the garden of Gethsemane on the night of His betrayal, He sweat drops of blood. The pressure was so intense the corpuscles on His forehead broke open. That was some serious pressure! The word *gethsemane* comes from the Hebrew words *gat shemanim*, which mean "olive press." An olive press was used to squeeze olives in order to make olive oil. It's interesting that Jesus's favorite place to pray in the city of Jerusalem was a place of pressing. Again—if you want to find Jesus, you can find Him in the press, right in the midst of your season of pressure, trauma, and loss. Consider these biblical passages about resilience in the midst of life's pressures:

> You know that under pressure, your faith-life is forced into the open and shows its true colors. (James 1:3 MSG)

> In pressure thou hast enlarged me. (Ps. 4:1 DARBY)

> If you fail under pressure,
>   your strength is too small. (Prov. 24:10 NLT)

Yes, it's true! The strength and power of a living God dwelling inside of you will enable you to withstand the pressures of life. You may be pressed on every side, but if you trust in Jesus you will not be crushed. The pressure of difficult circumstances enlarges faith. You were created for resilience. Yes, like ol' Tigger, you were fearfully and wonderfully made with a top made out of rubber and a bottom made out of springs!

BOUNCE TAKEAWAY:
Reflect on Your Own Story

1. Have you ever concluded that you don't have the capacity to live a resilient life? If so, what do you think caused you to accept this belief?

2. We just learned that we all have the same capacity for resilience. How does this knowledge change your outlook about your future?

3. We also discovered in this chapter that pressure is actually a positive thing that helps us to grow and mature. How has this truth changed your perspective on how you should respond to seasons of great difficulty?

BOUNCE CHALLENGE #2

One of the things I say in this chapter is, "Let me be clear: in order to press on regardless of the pressures and losses of life, you're going to need a supernatural, holy God indwelling your spirit." Before we can move on from this point in our study of resilience, it will be necessary for your success to make sure the life of Jesus fills your heart. Please reread two key passages from this chapter (2 Cor. 1:8–10 and 2 Cor. 4:8–11, 16–17) and afterward pen a prayer in your bounce journal that opens your heart fully to Jesus. Here is an example:

Lord Jesus, I open my heart to you today. Forgive me for hidden and outward sins that have left me feeling empty on the inside. I ask You to be the Lord of my life. Fill my soul with Your love and Your wonderful mercy and grace. I cannot go on without You in my life, Jesus. Thank you, Jesus, for living inside of me. I know that because of Your salvation I will never be crushed, perplexed, in despair, forsaken, or destroyed. Amen.

3

Reframe Your Loss

I would hope that some greatness might be left in you.
They say that crippled men have compensations which
make them stronger than the strong.

John Steinbeck, *Burning Bright*

On a blustery cold winter night in December 1914, a sixty-seven-year-old entrepreneur stood outside his factory buildings in West Orange, New Jersey, as massive flames engulfed the structures and climbed high into the frigid air. The two fire departments he had stationed inside the enormous complex were no threat to the inferno. He had designed and built the factory out of concrete and believed it could not be destroyed by fire.

Because he never thought it would happen to him, and that his concrete factory was invincible, he was woefully underinsured. The man's fortune was disappearing before his eyes.

While the fire raged on, his son Charles found him staring at the flames. Charles would later recall that his father told him to find his mother and bring her and her friends to see the flames, because, "She will never see anything like this as long as she lives!" The next morning, as the man picked through the ruins of his life's work, he said, "There is great value in disaster. All our mistakes are burned up. Thank God we can start anew!"

This man had learned to treat triumph and tragedy alike. Because he framed loss in its proper context, he could face this harrowing drama and survive to see his dreams fulfilled. He had learned that loss is a part of life. He had learned that disaster has some redeeming qualities: all of his mistakes were burned up. Oh, and before I forget, I should tell you the man's name: Thomas Edison.

The fire started in his film processing laboratory and destroyed valuable records and prototypes of his coming products. Three weeks after the tragic fire, having moved his fifteen hundred employees to temporary buildings nearby, Edison began rebuilding his company.

Edison continued to face obstacles. In 1917 America declared war on Germany, the main producer of a certain chemical Edison needed to develop the records that played on the phonograph he had invented years earlier. To solve this problem, Edison experimented with different ways of synthesizing the chemical and worked tirelessly until he discovered a solution. The first new plant Edison built after the tragic fire was for the production of this chemical so the world could hear beautiful music in a time of war. Soon, Edison's new factory would be manufacturing over a ton of the product every day.

Eye of the Beholder

I sometimes search for discarded oil paintings in resale shops. Generally, the paintings are unframed and worn with age. The passing of time has not ignored them. Leaking roofs and coal-burning stoves have contributed their fair share of erosion, cracks, and soot that mask the hidden hues just below the distress. Sight is repeatedly blind to their beauty, but I see a masterpiece.

So does my friend Chip, an art restorer and frame shop owner. Chip has taught me that frames add depth and dimension to works of art. You can place two identical paintings in separate frames, one plastic and the other rich wood, and the paintings will look completely different. Maybe we need to reframe loss. Put a new spin on it. Dust it off and give it a second look. Maybe loss is not the evil villain we've made it out to be.

The Drama of Loss

Loss is no respecter of persons. The real stuff of life is not what happens to us but how we react to it. Like being forced onto a stage unprepared to give a speech before thousands, loss can be shocking and humiliating in its sudden impact. Rarely are we fully prepared for the emotional drama that comes with loss. A kind of gray desolation ensues and the slightest whisper of hope is a mere distant echo, ricocheting off the person you once thought you were before this whole business of tragic disappointment began. There you stand on the stage, alone, wondering what to do and what to say. You secretly hope some merciful soul in the audience will pitch you a line or two.

For most, the drama of loss is just bad theater. If an appraisal of the painful excursion were ever penned, I'm convinced loss would have its fair share of critics. I doubt there would be many five-star ratings in loss's favor. No two enthusiastic thumbs-up. No syrupy, glowing accolades. No rave reviews.

Yet maybe we have it all wrong. Maybe we've turned good theater into bad simply because we've made loss an unwelcome guest—an old, irritable, unpredictable, socially awkward relative we are ashamed to admit has our blood hobbling through his or her arteries. This visitor seems destined to remind us of our collective past: the difficult days following 9/11, the financial collapse in 2008, the uncertainty of our times.

The person who understands loss speaks of tragedy and blessing together in one sentence as if the two are acquainted, having learned through adversity that loss, if properly framed, can be a blessing even in the pain.

Back in 1961, famous author John Steinbeck drove a pickup truck across the American landscape with his dog, Charley. Steinbeck confessed that he had felt out of touch with his country for twenty-five years and wanted to reconnect. The stories of his travel are recorded in his classic book *Travels with Charley: In Search of America*. In a letter to his editor about his journey, Steinbeck says:

> In all my travels I saw very little real poverty, I mean the grinding terrifying poorness of the Thirties. That at least was real and tangible. No, it was a sickness, a kind of wasting disease. There were wishes but no wants. And underneath it all the building energy like gases in a corpse. When that explodes, I tremble to think what will be the result. Over and over I thought we lack the pressures that make men strong and the anguish that makes men great.[1]

Perhaps, because of the almost unbroken prosperity our nation has enjoyed for over fifty years, we as individuals have outgrown the need for a good jolt of loss every now and then. Our wealth has allowed us to discard the concept altogether. But with a world economy on the brink—when people are out of work around the globe and retirees are reentering the workforce because of tanking retirement portfolios—it might be a good idea to rediscover loss, reframe it, and rethink it.

My friend Tom Arrington owns a large pharmaceutical company in Cincinnati, Ohio. As all businessmen know, Tom understands that loss is a part of business. Yet, for Tom, loss is a welcome teacher. A dynamic Christian leader, Tom makes lots of great quips about life and business. My favorite? "Some days I win and other days I learn." Through years of leading a great company with a Christian worldview, Tom sees the value of the education that loss brings to the table. He has learned to reframe loss as learning, as valuable experience.

The Stages of Loss

I have spoken with many people who are in different stages of loss. Some are dealing with financial loss. Others have lost dreams. Some have seen businesses they built over a lifetime collapse. Others are dealing with the loss of a loved one through death. Some parents are facing the loss of children through suicide. Each person has one thing in common, a theme that unites them: they all confess that in the midst of their great losses they have never felt more alive or closer to God. Like an unexpected, sharp, and jabbing pain that blows every substation in our central nervous system with the speed of a lightning bolt, loss has a way of letting us know that we're still human and still very much alive.

When you think about it, many of the notable defining moments of your life occur in times of pain. C. S. Lewis said, "Pain insists upon being attended to. God whispers to us in our pleasures, speaks in our consciousness, but shouts in our pains. It is His megaphone to rouse a deaf world."[2] I find it compelling how hard it is to forget what pains we had in a time of loss, yet how much harder still it is to remember what joys we had in a time of gain. The discomfort we endure in loss forms the costly pearls in our character. We have no victory crowns to show for bliss. Gain gets all the good press, but in the end it's your loss you hold dear, since it is your best teacher.

Gain isn't all it's cracked up to be. That's why the apostle Paul, writing to the church in Philippi, could say:

> But what things were gain to me, these I have counted loss for Christ. Yet indeed I also count all things loss for the excellence of the knowledge of Christ Jesus my Lord, for whom I have suffered

the loss of all things, and count them as rubbish, that I may gain Christ. (Phil. 3:7–8)

Paul found the meaning of framing his losses in the right context. Compared to the depth of gaining Christ, any gain in this world, no matter how grand, was a loss. Maybe this is why Paul never feared bad news. Maybe it's why his faith never crumbled under pressure. What can you possibly take from a man who has nothing to lose?

Hebrews 11:3 tells us, "By faith we understand that the worlds were framed by the word of God, so that the things which are seen were not made of things which are visible." The Greek word for "framed" in this passage is *katartizo*, and it simply means "to put in order." We need to frame our losses in their proper order, in their right context. The story of God, the great drama of the Bible, is framed in the context of loss. God made the world and everything in it and called it good: paradise created. After sin entered the world through Adam, all of God's creation became corrupted: paradise lost.

The most tragic figure in the entire Bible is God Himself. No one has endured more painful and tragic loss than He. God lost a planet; the whole world is under the control of the evil one. God lost a garden. God lost intimacy with the first family made in His image. God the Father has endured the pain of extreme loss. The entire biblical narrative from Genesis to Revelation portrays the great drama of God's losses and His passionate work of redemption and restoration. The pinnacle of the story revolves around the person of Jesus, the One who came to seek and to save that which is lost.

The parables of Jesus portray the Father's unyielding commitment to recover His losses: the lost son, the lost coin, and the lost sheep are stories revealing that when something or someone is lost, God never counts it as a loss. He does not frame it that way. At the end of the biblical drama we see Jesus, the Lamb of God, made worthy through His suffering standing before the Father and receiving the title deed of planet earth—paradise restored!

What is so amazing about this entire drama of paradise created, paradise lost, and paradise restored is that God the Father had prepared for the loss before the world even began. God was not alarmed when His creation was corrupted. Loss was not a surprise intruder. God had expected its arrival all along. We know this because the Bible teaches that Jesus's sacrifice for sin was carried out before the very foundation of the world.

God designed a recovery before He incurred loss. I don't know why God allowed sin to enter into the world in the first place. Perhaps it is because the same God who framed the present world in the context of loss and redemption is the God who has designed the world to come. And that world is for those willing to be redeemed from the losses sin has imparted in this life. Surely, the weighty magnitude of the songs of the saints in heaven will be the depth of their thanksgiving. If there were no sin to conquer, no service to be rendered to the King, no marks or wounds from the spiritual warfare that rages, no suffering for righteousness, no losses or pain encountered, the redeemed would live eternally shy of a testimony. We would exist without living because to be alive is to have scars. The songs of the heavenly redeemed will be about victories won, wounds healed, tears transformed into unbelievable joy, and losses restored.

Suffering Breeds Compassion

Between 1942 and 1945 Viktor Frankl labored in four different Nazi death camps, including Auschwitz. His pregnant wife, brother, and parents all died within the camps. In the foreword to Viktor Frankl's book *Man's Search for Meaning*, Rabbi Harold Kushner discusses his theories:

> Life is not primarily a quest for pleasure . . . but a quest for meaning . . . Suffering in and of itself is meaningless; we give our suffering

meaning by the way in which we respond to it . . . [a person] may remain brave, dignified and unselfish, or in the bitter fight for self-preservation he may forget his human dignity and become no more than an animal. . . . Forces beyond your control can take away everything you possess except one thing, your freedom to choose how you will respond to the situation. You cannot control what happens to you in life, but you can always control what you will feel and do about what happens to you.[3]

Frankl (and Kushner) are right. In our bitter fight for self-preservation, we have forgotten the core pillars of our human dignity: empathy and compassion. The driving ambition to protect ourselves from loss has in reality erased meaning and purpose from our lives. We have become austere, detached, and indifferent toward the burdens others bear. Like a dry reservoir, our emotions have been drained of sympathy by a kind of barren unfeeling.

I have always thought the Good Samaritan was compassionate because he, too, had experienced rejection and violence. Without the sting of loss, we may just go on living unscathed by human need, oblivious to others' pain because we've never experienced it. I think more than changing things about us, loss reveals things within us. It uncovers the hideous creatures of pride, arrogance, and self-centeredness lurking in the dark corridors of our souls. That's why in the midst of a losing season we feel very much alive. God has designed the trial to bring out the best in us, the real dignity of who we are. He is challenging our minds to reveal what's in our hearts.

A New Perspective

Without a doubt, enduring the drama that loss creates is painful. Emotional pain is overwhelming in these times. Physical trauma is also painful, but a backache never quite reaches the intensity of a broken spirit. Questions abound during seasons of loss, such as, "Will I ever come through this?" "Will I be standing, when and if I do?" "Will there be anything left of me when this is all over?" "How will the pain of this loss affect my family?" "Has God forgotten me?" "Is God concerned about me?" If you have recently experienced loss, I am certain you have been crying out to God with questions similar to these.

Now is your moment to reframe your perspective of loss. Start looking at loss as the great teacher God destined it to be. Embrace it and come back to the land of the living. Like the leaping and cascading flames of Edison's factory fire, you may not see anything like this as long as you live. This is not the end of a thing but the beginning. This may well be the clearest defining moment of your life.

BOUNCE TAKEAWAY:
Reflect on Your Own Story

1. As you look back over your life, which has taught you the most about yourself: pain or pleasure?
2. When you think about loss, do you view it as an unwelcome intruder or a welcome teacher?
3. As you think about the possibility of bouncing back from your losses, which one of these is your goal?

   1. To quickly recover from this loss and be back on top again.
   2. To learn some things about yourself in the midst of the loss and pain, no matter how long the process takes.

   How you answer this question is significant because it will determine your ability to face the next loss, failure, or heartache that comes your way.

BOUNCE CHALLENGE #3

In your journal, I would like for you to write down five things you desire to learn from this season of loss and heartache. Here are a few examples:

1. I want the sting of loss to make me more compassionate toward others who are suffering setbacks.
2. I want this season of loss to uncover who I really am and reveal to me what I'm actually made of.

4

The Little-Known Story of C. W. Baston

It was only when I lay there on rotting prison straw
that I sensed within myself the first stirrings of good.
Gradually, it was disclosed to me that the line sepa-
rating good and evil passes not through states, nor
between classes, nor between political parties either—
but right through every human heart—and through
all human hearts. . . . I nourished my soul there, and
I say without hesitation: Bless you, prison, for having
been in my life.

Alexander Solzhenitsyn, *The Gulag Archipelago*

Down in the low country lies the Wiregrass region of Alabama.
Unremarkable farm towns dot the landscape. One town,
Enterprise, has made its way into American history. It is the only
place in the world that has built a statue in honor of a deadly bug.

Back in 1892 a merciless agricultural terminator known as the
boll weevil beetle migrated across the Rio Grande from Mexico
into Texas. The boll weevil feeds on cotton buds, causing the

39

cotton to yellow and eventually rot. In those days cotton was the cash crop of Southern farmers. The entire Southern economy was built on the production and exportation of cotton.

For the next thirty years the boll weevil spread across the Southern cotton belt, leaving in its wake destruction, poverty, bankruptcy, and loss. Many of the folk songs of this era were written about the boll weevil and its annihilation of rural cotton farming communities across the South.

The boll weevil munched away, and by 1915 it had reached the state of Alabama. The effect on the state's cotton production was devastating. By the end of 1917, Alabama had suffered a 70 percent loss of its cotton crop. In 1914, the year before the boll weevil arrived, Alabama harvested more than 1.7 million bales of cotton. In 1917, a mere half million bales were produced.

Famous Tuskegee University is ninety miles north of Enterprise. In those days, an agricultural scientist at Tuskegee was studying crop rotation and diversification as a way to save rural farmers from the boll weevil. This professor theorized that growing peanuts and other crops would stop the advance of the vicious invader. In 1916, he published one of his many bulletins to help the Southern farmer, entitled "How to Grow the Peanut and 105 Ways of Preparing It for Human Consumption." The recipes included peanut soup, peanut bread, peanut cookies, peanut wafers, peanut doughnuts, peanut patties, peanut stuffing, peanut salad, and even peanut omelets. For the sweet tooth he included peanut ice cream and peanut frappes. And let's not forget about peanut butter!

A former slave, this professor knew what incurring loss was all about. As a child, he was separated from his mother and sisters, never to see them again. His name, of course, is Dr. George Washington Carver. But in 1916 not many were interested in Dr. Carver's unproven theories. Farmers only knew how to plant and harvest cotton. Cotton was king, not peanuts! Besides, what region would ever want to be known for peanuts anyway?

What's that great definition of insanity? Doing the same thing over again and expecting different results. One year after suffering the obliteration of 60 percent of their cotton crop, the farmers of Enterprise planted cotton again.

All except for one. His name was C. W. Baston. Once a proud and prominent farmer, now he was on the verge of losing everything to bankruptcy. Baston was up to his ears in debt to a local banker and cotton merchant named H. M. Sessions.

In a twist of fate, Sessions had been studying Dr. Carver's theories about growing peanuts in the Wiregrass and made an interesting proposal to Baston: if he would dedicate the next season to growing peanuts on his land, the bank would provide the peanut seed and the workers to harvest the crop and would pay one dollar for every bushel of peanuts grown. It was an unproven idea, but another year of the powerful boll weevil might sink Sessions's bank.

The offer was accepted, and that year, 1916, C. W. Baston became the only farmer growing peanuts in Coffee County, Alabama. He produced eight thousand bushels of peanuts, and the bank paid him eight thousand dollars—enough to pay his entire debt with some left over. When the other farmers saw Baston's success, they came to him to purchase peanut seed for the next growing season. In 1917, Coffee County produced more than one million bushels of peanuts that were sold on the market for over five million dollars. They say the peanut yield that year was so incredible that every vacant building in Enterprise was filled with peanuts! By 1919, Coffee County, Alabama, was the number one producer of peanuts in the United States. A former slave, a dried-up banker, and a broke farmer changed history with a risky idea that went against a hundred years of tradition. Within two years, the region would dedicate four million acres to peanut cultivation.

On December 11, 1919, a statue of a woman in a flowing gown, shipped all the way from Italy, was erected in the city square of Enterprise, Alabama. Three thousand people came to see her unveiling. They even had a band. The invited keynote speaker was none other than Dr. George Washington Carver, although he was unable to attend as heavy rains had washed out the railroad track from Tuskegee. C. W. Baston was there and so was H. M. Sessions. The arms of the woman stretch heavenward, lifting a trophy to the sky. On top of the trophy is a larger-than-life boll weevil beetle, and at the base of the statue are these striking words:

BOLL WEEVIL MONUMENT
December 11, 1919
In profound appreciation of the Boll Weevil and what it has done as the Herald of Prosperity
This monument was erected by the Citizens of Enterprise, Coffee County, Alabama

In the face of impending doom, the good citizens of Enterprise learned the remarkable lesson of bouncing back. They found a silver lining in their tragic circumstances. In the process, they saw their greatest adversary as their greatest teacher, an agent of change. They thanked the ruthless boll weevil for forcing their decision to risk something new. Their story is used today in technology, medical research, and business philosophy as a prime example of problem solving through a willingness to change strategy and diversify when facing loss and adversity.

Three Critical Questions

Perhaps the fairy-tale ending to C. W. Baston's story makes his decision to accept loss and move on seem simple. Yet when you think about the deep-rooted cotton culture of the Wiregrass region in 1916, planting peanuts was like a forbidden sin. Because of his losses, Baston had already suffered enough humiliation. So why would he want to risk becoming the laughingstock of Coffee

County by planting peanuts? For Baston to make this giant leap of faith and diversify his crop, he had to ask himself three questions:

Can visions die?

Can I accept my loss?

What have I learned because of my loss?

If you are willing to ask yourself these three questions and answer them honestly, you, too, have a chance to bounce back from loss!

Can Visions Die?

Can a God-given life vision die? We struggle with this question because when our vision was launched, we made decisions and sacrifices, invested time and money, and took extreme care to see the vision through to completion. We did our best. We thought through the possibilities of failure as best we could. We believed God was leading us. But now the vision is dormant or dying, and we are suffering because we don't know what is happening. The humiliation of it all stings because we have made promises we cannot keep. Not only is our dream dying but our reputation and integrity are being buried in the sands of loss as well.

Can visions die? In history, whomever God called suffered the death of the very vision God gave them. Abraham received the promised vision that he would be a great nation. Twenty-five years later, God required he take his promised son to be sacrificed on an altar. We know from the story that God provided a lamb to replace Isaac. Even though Abraham believed God would raise Isaac from the dead should he die on that mound of stones, still tears must have been running down the old man's beard as he raised the knife in the air toward his beloved boy's heart.

Consider Joseph, who dreamed of being a great leader and soon afterward was cast into a pit. From there he was pushed deeper into indentured slavery and was finally thrown even further down into a prison dungeon. More than seventeen years of agony would pass before his life vision was resurrected from the abyss of despair. The psalmist picks up on the reason for the death of a vision when he writes of Joseph's agony, "They hurt his feet with fetters, he was laid in irons. Until the time that his word came to pass, the word of the LORD tested him" (Ps. 105:18–19).

Moses was given a vision from God to free the Israelites from four hundred years under Egyptian bondage. Almost as soon as it was born, that vision died and Moses would spend forty years as a shepherd before God rekindled the dream in his heart. Saul of Tarsus (later Paul) met Jesus face-to-face on the Damascus Road and heard a message that would radically alter his future. The Lord Jesus imparted a worldwide vision to Paul that would lead him to preach the gospel to the gentile nations. But first, Paul spent the next fourteen years in obscurity.

Why does God allow life visions He gives to us to temporarily die? He is testing us in the setbacks and losses of life in order to prepare us to shepherd the immense dream He has birthed within us. If you are suffering the death pangs of a God-given vision, a designated day of redemption is in your future. When a vision is dormant or dead, the enemy of your soul tries to convince you that you were never meant to live that dream. But God allows a vision to die so that you will trust in His abilities. It takes faith to see a life vision birthed. It takes greater faith to let the vision go, believing God will restore it in His time.

To answer the question, "Can visions die?" God's Word says, "Most assuredly, I say to you, unless a grain of wheat falls into the ground and dies, it remains alone; but if it dies, it produces much grain" (John 12:24). One way or the other, God is going to refine you. God is concerned about what happens to you. But He is more intimately and deeply concerned about what happens in you. Can visions die? Yes, they can.

Can I Accept Loss?

Job asked this question in his epic book about suffering loss: "Shall we indeed accept good from God, and shall we not accept adversity?" (Job 2:10). Job saw his loss as an act of a sovereign God who brings to each of us both triumph and adversity, pain and pleasure. Can you face your loss and see the hand of God in it? Can you accept loss?

After David committed adultery with Bathsheba, the wife of Uriah, David was confronted by Nathan the prophet and repented of his sin. Bathsheba became pregnant and gave birth to a son. The child became ill, and David fasted and prayed for seven days for the life of the boy. On the seventh day the child died, and David's reaction is an extraordinary example of how one can accept loss, no matter how painful:

> Then on the seventh day it came to pass that the child died. And the servants of David were afraid to tell him that the child was dead. For they said, "Indeed, while the child was alive, we spoke to him, and he would not heed our voice. How can we tell him that the child is dead? He may do some harm!"
>
> When David saw that his servants were whispering, David perceived that the child was dead. Therefore David said to his servants, "Is the child dead?"
>
> And they said, "He is dead."
>
> So David arose from the ground, washed and anointed himself, and changed his clothes; and he went into the house of the LORD and worshiped. Then he went to this own house; and when he requested, they set food before him, and he ate. Then his servants said to him, "What is this that you have done? You fasted and wept for the child while he was alive, but when the child died, you arose and ate food."
>
> And he said, "While the child was alive, I fasted and wept; for I said, 'Who can tell whether the LORD will be gracious to me, that the child may live? But now he is dead; why should I fast? Can I bring him back again? I shall go to him, but he shall not return to me.'" (2 Sam. 12:18–23)

Think of it. David committed adultery and orchestrated the death of Bathsheba's husband. His sins of adultery and murder had placed his entire family in peril. Often, the consequences of such sins are suffering and loss. We should always examine our hearts and repent as David did if we have departed from God's commandments. After repentance and cleansing, it's also vitally important that we don't allow shame to enter our hearts. People tend to hold on to the baggage of their past sins. David didn't. He accepted the fact his tragic loss was due to his own sin, got up from the ground, and went to the temple to worship God. He decided not to live in shame and declared that living in remorse over his loss was not going to bring the child back. David decided to go on living. Of course, not every loss is a result of sin, but even so, people tend to hold on to the pain of their losses, thinking that somehow their self-condemnation will change their circumstances.

One of my favorite passages of Scripture about the need to bounce back after suffering loss is in 2 Chronicles. A young king of Judah, Amaziah, was going to war against the Edomites. To prepare for battle he hired one hundred thousand mighty men of valor from Israel to the tune of one hundred talents of silver (about $1.6 million in today's dollars). A man of God came to the king and told him that hiring these soldiers was a very bad idea. But Amaziah had already paid the soldiers a lot of money and was having a hard time accepting that he would lose and that he should dismiss them from the battle. Amaziah asked the man of God a direct question about incurring loss, and the answer has helped me on numerous occasions to accept my losses and place my faith in a God who is ever willing to restore my deficits and give me full restitution.

> Then Amaziah said to the man of God, "But what shall we do about the hundred talents which I have given to the troops of Israel?"
> And the man of God answered, "The LORD is able to give you much more than this." (2 Chron. 25:9)

46

One of the great tragedies in modern-day Christians is that we are losing our ability to rebound, to summon the sheer determination to come back from defeat. Yes, we may suffer some setbacks, but we should never be defeated. If we lose faith in the fact that God's love is perfect and His wisdom is infallible, and neither can be improved upon, we will never be able to accept our losses. We will ultimately doubt that what is happening to us in this season of loss is somehow all part of God's sovereign plan. When our faith is low, a high level of fear fills the void. Next, shame slithers into our thoughts and leaves in its wake confusion, humiliation, self-hatred, and self-loathing. Unending questions such as *Why did I make that decision?* invade our consciousness. We see ourselves as the proverbial village idiot and believe that others view us as the same or even worse.

Here is a piece of information you may not have considered: there are many other people in this world who have suffered great losses as well. When you initially suffer loss, a time of reflection is healthy, but endlessly second-guessing your past decisions will cloud your present decisiveness. If you see all of life's losses as negatives—if loss is unacceptable to you—you won't learn much from it. Loss affects each and every one of us. The question is, can you accept it as a part of life and bounce back?

What Have I Learned?

What is all of this adversity teaching us? I don't necessarily believe God allows loss in order to change us as much as to unveil us. When we stumble, we find out where we really stand. I have learned a few things from my losses. First of all, loss is temporary. You're going to get through this. The old adage "This too shall pass" is not just a frivolous bon mot.

Second, loss is necessary. Ecclesiastes makes this clear: "To everything there is a season, a time for every purpose under heaven . . . a time to gain, and a time to lose" (Eccles. 3:1, 6). The winter season, though cold and sometimes brutal, kills off many of the insects and pests that would lower crop yields at harvest time.

Third, loss brings clarity. First Corinthians 3:15 states, "If anyone's work is burned, he will suffer loss; but he himself will be saved, yet so as through fire." Loss has an uncanny way of defining and clarifying our values and motivations. Consider this: when Israel was under the dominion of the Persian empire, for the most part the Jewish people learned to blend in to the culture of their conquerors. Under Persian rule, the Jews built wealth and security for themselves. According to Jewish history, God sent forty-eight prophets and seven prophetesses to Persia to call Israel to repentance. Nothing had an effect on them until King Ahasuerus removed his signet ring and gave it to evil Haman, who planned on annihilating all of the Jews of Persia. The prophets pled with the Jews and their behavior didn't change. But when the king removed his signet ring, the gravity of the situation finally dawned on them. When we face loss, could it be that God has been trying to get through to us and we are not listening? You see, loss brings everything into focus, unveils our hearts, and redefines our values. Ultimately, loss is a mercy. In allowing a temporary loss that brings us back to Him, God in His mercy is preventing us from suffering long-term destruction and loss.

■ ■ ■

Can visions die? Can I accept loss? What am I learning? The right answers to these three questions can drastically alter your future. C. W. Baston realized that cotton would no longer be his crop of choice—for him, his way of life. He accepted the reality of the boll weevil's ruthless migration across his land and his inability to block its path. He learned from Dr. George Washington Carver that crop diversification was the only way to save his farm. After an honest assessment of his circumstances, he planted peanut seed and saved the family farm, the town of Enterprise, Coffee County, the Wiregrass region, and ultimately the entire economy of the

South. It took a well-respected farmer taking a big risk in order to begin to change the thinking of an entire region of farmers.

And oh, by the way, if you're ever in the Wiregrass region of the Deep South, be sure to drop by the town square in Enterprise, because the boll weevil statue still stands there today.

BOUNCE TAKEAWAY:
Reflect on Your Own Story

1. As you look back over your past, what moment stands out to you as a time when, in the midst of a loss, you recalibrated your approach to the problem, tried something new, and ultimately bounced back?
2. Why do you think the cotton farmers in Coffee County, Alabama, initially responded negatively to planting peanuts? Have you ever been hesitant to try a new thing even when you knew it was the right thing to do?
3. Resilience requires change. Is there anything in you presently that resists the changes you need to make? If so, what is causing you to be hesitant?

 BOUNCE CHALLENGE #4

In our last journal entry we wrote down five things we desired our heartache to teach us. Now, let's simplify it. I would like you to write these words in your bounce journal:

In my journey through this season of loss, one important thing I am learning so far is: (try to express this one thing in a short paragraph).

PART 2

The Four Resilience Blockers

5

Self-Pity

The Pain of Your Past Is Actually the Canvas of Your Future Masterpiece

> No, no. Then we must treat it just the same as we
> would treat a triumph, madam. Is that not what your
> Mr. Kipling tells us? Although, of course, here we
> have a problem, because I, Sunil Indrajit Kapoor, have
> never had a triumph. So, of course, I do not know
> how to treat one. No, all I've had is a constant series
> of disasters interspersed with occasional catastrophe.
>
> Dev Patel, *The Best Exotic Marigold Hotel*

St. Andrews in Scotland has the unique and prestigious honor of being the world's oldest golf club. The Royal Calcutta Golf Club, built in 1829 in Calcutta, India, has the distinct pleasure of being the world's second oldest golf club. Originally located near Dum Dum Airport (now Netaii Sobhash Chandra Bose

International Airport), in 1910 it moved to its present location at Tollygunge. The course was christened with the title "Royal" by King George V and Queen Mary during their visit in 1911. As British colonialism expanded in Southern Asia, the English longed for the lifestyle an exclusive club could offer. On the fairways and greens of a proper gentleman's club, where competition, rules, and penalties would offer a dash of European order to men far from home, the Royal Calcutta Golf Club magically imported first-world sense and sensibilities to the third. And with it—perfection.

But soon after opening, as the story goes (it's possibly just a tall tale, but a wonderful one), there were problems at the Royal Calcutta Golf Club. No, the aged imported brandy had not run out. The hot towels in the barber shop were still at just the most delightful and soothing temperature. Shoe shiners were still polishing and crumpets were still being served for high tea. Actually, everything at the Royal Calcutta Golf Club was in Royal British order. In fact, the whole affair would have been a smashing success—if it weren't for the monkeys.

The one thing the Brits didn't consider when the Royal Calcutta was being planned and constructed was that the golf course was surrounded by a heavily wooded forest inhabited by wild monkeys. When the proper British gentlemen, dressed in their ironed knickers and sporting their waxed handlebar mustaches, drove the golf balls down the fairway, the monkeys would spring from the forest, rush across the unblemished, freshly mowed grass, pick up the balls, and scramble about for a bit in wild monkey fashion before screaming back to the safety of their habitat, leaving golf balls everywhere except where the players had hit them. Where was the British sense and sensibility in any of this?

So the game at the Royal Calcutta Golf Club, having lost all symmetry and dignity due to an untidy and unfortunate series of events, was ruined. Wild monkeys posed an existential threat to its very propriety.

Oh, it's not like the Brits gave in so easily to their monkey problem. They actually tried everything. They built fences around the fairways, but the monkeys climbed over them. They blew whistles to scare the monkeys away, but the sounds only acted like Hans Christian Anderson's Pied Piper and attracted more monkeys. They even hired people to act like monkeys and roam through the trees shouting. No, that didn't work either. The monkeys kept menacing the members of the Royal Calcutta Golf Club by enthusiastically mocking European dignity. They displaced golf balls from one side of the fairway to the other. They rankled scorekeepers and rule keepers because you just can't go moving golf balls once they're in play. It's just not respectable.

So, as the story goes, the Royal Calcutta Golf Club did the only thing a respectable club could do: they changed the rules of the game. Instead of being consumed by self-pity, the club dared to stare defeat in the face and found a way around its problem.

Would you like to know, as the story goes, what the new official rule was? Here it is: "Play the ball where the monkey dropped it."

The Brits realized there was no way to get rid of their monkey problem, so they embraced it. The problem that is, not the monkeys. Golf courses are filled with hazards like sand and water traps, so what are a few monkeys anyway? Besides, if the monkey dropped your ball closer to the hole it would work out in your favor. But, of course, if the monkey dropped it farther away from the hole or in the rough, you might be penalized by the monkey's behavior. So to make it fair for every player, the standing rule was to play the ball where the monkey dropped it. I don't know if it's true or not, but legend has it one player used the new rule to his advantage by training a monkey to drop his ball into the hole. Hole in one!

In this life, we all have our monkeys, hazards, and pitfalls. When things don't go the way we planned and all our best efforts to build a splendid and orderly Royal Calcutta Golf Club are dashed by a surprising handful of wild monkeys, how do we respond? How do we deal with it when our perfect, orderly world is upended by things out of our control?

Rather than allowing the agitation of loss and setback to bring us to a place of self-pity, I would suggest we take advice from the old-world sensibility of the Royal Calcutta Golf Club and just play the ball where the monkey dropped it. That's true resilience. That's pressing on regardless.

The Most Sinister of Roadblocks

I call self-pity the first roadblock to resilience because it is the most sinister. Loss leaves in its wake a good deal of emotional turmoil and pain, so it's easy to be led into self-pity's trap. Why? Because it's really hard to distinguish between normal emotional pain and the gentle lure of self-pity. Succumbing to that gentle downward-spiraling vortex is kind of like falling asleep: slowly at first, and all of a sudden, you're dreaming.

You can liken the enchanting whisper of self-pity to the song of the sirens in Homer's *Odyssey*. Many a vessel and its crew had been driven onto the rocks, drawn by the subtle and seductive melodies of the sirens. To save his ship from destruction, Odysseus ordered his men to plug their ears with beeswax to mute the sirens' songs and to keep them from rowing toward the rocks. Like the sirens, self-pity is equally cunning, inviting, and, yes, destructive.

Self-pity is, well, selfish. It demands your full attention and becomes fiercely jealous when you entertain thoughts of resilience. The hideous intention of self-pity is to become your chief counselor. It will eviscerate any reasonable voice from the depths of your soul that desires to view your loss with a balanced perspective. Self-pity eventually destroys every way of thinking except, of course, its own. Self-pity gains power quickly because it's the path of least resistance.

You see, when a person suffers a setback it's comforting to believe the real culprit is unfairness. It's easy to start believing that if you were just given a better chance things would be different. Once you start entertaining thoughts of self-pity, you get trapped in a revolving door going around and around what might have been if you hadn't suffered loss. The result is spiritual, emotional, and mental stagnation. And guess what? At that point, self-pity is just getting started. Its thirst for control is not fully quenched until it draws a crowd. The old adage "misery loves company" describes self-pity's ultimate nirvana: drawing family and close friends into its paralyzing web. There, honey-filled cinnamon-sprinkled morsels of sympathy are served up daily to your tortured soul. In this surreal state of existence, the pity party just expands. Pretty soon family and close friends start seeing the world through your warped view; before long they start pitying themselves as well.

The whole idea of self-pity is rooted in deception, and we would do well to heed the simple wisdom of this line from the movie *The Princess Bride*: "Life is pain, Highness. Anyone who says differently is selling something."[1]

So Old, It Started in Eden

Self-pity is not a new kid on the block. It's an ancient roadblock that attempts to squelch any and all resistance and has existed relatively unchallenged by multitudes for millennia. The first place we see the cunning tactics of self-pity is in the Garden of Eden. After the original sin of eating the forbidden fruit, Adam and Eve hid themselves from God in shame because they realized for the first time they were naked. We pick up the scene in Genesis 3:

> Then the Lord God called to Adam and said to him, "Where are you?"
> So he said, "I heard Your voice in the garden, and I was afraid because I was naked; and I hid myself."

And He said, "Who told you that you were naked? Have you eaten from the tree of which I commanded you that you should not eat?"

Then the man said, "The woman whom You gave to be with me, she gave me of the tree, and I ate." (Gen. 3:9–12)

One of the fruits of self-pity is blame-shifting. Adam not only cast the shadow of blame over his wife but he also accused God in the same sentence: "The woman whom You gave to be with me." Adam was basically saying, "If there's any victim here, it's me. God, you're responsible for getting me into this mess. I was doing just fine until you brought this woman into the garden, and she actually sinned in the first place by picking the fruit. All I did was take a few bites." And so one of the first fruits of the fall of man, all the way back in the book of beginnings, was self-pity. Its seeds have produced a sizable harvest ever since.

We see self-pity surface again in the Jewish exodus from slavery in Egypt. As the people were poised to enter the Promised Land, Moses, directed by God, sent twelve men to survey their new homeland. When they returned, the majority were down on the place. Ten out of the twelve took the path of least resistance and any hope of resilience was blocked by self-pity. We pick up the story in Numbers 13:

And they gave the children of Israel a bad report of the land which they had spied out, saying, "The land through which we have gone as spies is a land that devours its inhabitants, and all the people whom we saw in it are men of great stature. There we saw the giants (the descendants of Anak came from the giants); and we were like grasshoppers in our own sight, and so we were in their sight."

So all the congregation lifted up their voices and cried, and the people wept that night. And all the children of Israel complained against Moses and Aaron, and the whole congregation said to them, "If only we had died in the land of Egypt! Or if only we had died in this wilderness! Why has the LORD brought us to this land to fall by the sword, that our wives and children should become victims? Would it not be better for us to return to Egypt?" So they said to one another, "Let us select a leader and return to Egypt." (Num. 13:32–14:4)

It has always puzzled me why self-pity earned the allegiance of the Israelites after all the miracles that had delivered them from Egypt. I mean, let's be honest: If God could part a sea, couldn't He deal with a few sniveling giants?

But then I realized life is full of misfortune and potholes and death, and kitchen tables stacked with unpaid bills, and grief, and suffering, and hotels with no vacancies, and cold dampness that seeps into your bones, and unexpected wild monkeys, and things so painful they take your breath away and leave you crying through the night.

And it dawned on me that with all the bumps along the way, a lot of people lose their childhood innocence and, with it, their resilience. It's just much easier, even comforting, to take the beeswax out of your ears and succumb to the gentle wooing of the sirens on the shore.

So how did God respond to Israel's self-pity? Did He soothe and comfort them, embracing their sense of victimization? On the contrary; He blocked them from entering the Promised Land, knowing that self-pity was so embedded in their thinking they had no ability to possess the land. It's absolutely stunning to realize it, but the thing that caused a nation to waste decades in the wilderness was unbelief inspired by self-pity. Challenging a people to leave the bondage of Egypt was actually easier for Moses than inspiring them to leave the bondage of self-pity.

The takeaway for me in this episode of Israel's history is that self-pity left a generation wandering in the wilderness, separated from their promise. It also brings me to the realization that self-focused, indulgent sympathy is not my friend but rather a destroyer of future promises and dreams.

Thirty-Eight Years Is Long Enough!

Most believe that Israel wandered in the wilderness for forty years. But in actuality it was thirty-eight years. Why the disparity, and why does it matter? We'll see why it matters when we learn of something that happened in Jesus's early ministry. But first, the disparity.

After leaving Egypt, the Israelites spent time at Mount Sinai, where they received the ten commandments and the law. From there they traveled to Kadesh Barnea to prepare to enter into the land of promise. For this large community, traveling from Sinai to Kadesh Barnea took a year. Then, after they rebelled against God and refused to possess their promised land, they wandered in the wilderness for thirty-eight years in self-pity. They later returned to Kadesh Barnea and prepared to enter into the land. This final process took another full year. So it was forty years total between leaving Egypt and crossing the Jordan into the land of promise, but only thirty-eight of those years were spent wandering. Deuteronomy 2:14 confirms this: "And the time we took to come from Kadesh Barnea until we crossed over the Valley of the Zered was thirty-eight years."

The story of Israel's thirty-eight-year wilderness sojourn is actually an opening act for what some consider to be Jesus's first major public miracle. The miracle I'm talking about is found in John 5 and it's known as the healing of the man at the Pool of Bethesda. To me, this miracle is one of the greatest examples in the Bible of the powerful force of self-pity and how to overcome it. Let's read about this miracle from John's Gospel.

> After this there was a feast of the Jews, and Jesus went up to Jerusalem. Now there is in Jerusalem by the Sheep Gate a pool, which

is called in Hebrew, Bethesda, having five porches. In these lay a great multitude of sick people, blind, lame, paralyzed, waiting for the moving of the water. For an angel went down at a certain time into the pool and stirred up the water, then whoever stepped in first, after the stirring of the water, was made well of whatever disease he had. (John 5:1–4)

As Jesus came up to Jerusalem for one of the feasts, He entered the city through the Sheep Gate. The sheep market was located here. As pilgrims came to worship at the temple, they would purchase a sacrificial lamb at the Sheep Gate and bring it to the temple for a burnt offering. Think of it: Jesus, the Lamb of God, came into Jerusalem through the gate of the lamb. By the gate there was a pool called Bethesda, surrounded by five columns. *Bethesda* means "house of mercy," and it was God's mercy for the broken that attracted to this pool hundreds, perhaps thousands, of people paralyzed with sickness, despair, disappointment, and self-pity. Some say an underground mineral spring fed the pool and this is what caused the stirring of the water and eventually the superstition of a healing angel. Others believe it was actually an angel who stirred the water. Either way, I can imagine the sick vying for position in order to be as close to the edge as possible.

I can also imagine Jesus walking through the gate of the lamb and passing through the sheep market. Did He think about His future, when He Himself would be the sacrificial lamb that would redeem the world from sin? I can see Him approaching Bethesda and fill with compassion for the multitude bound with despair. I'm sure His desire was to go to each person one by one and heal them. But He didn't. As Jesus passed through the stench of rotting humanity, He intentionally focused His gaze on one man. One unassuming guy in this collection of poor and pitiful souls caught Jesus's attention. And He walked right to him, most likely having to carefully navigate through the throng so as not to step on a paralyzed leg or crooked arm. I can see the anguished faces looking up at Him as He passed them by.

Why would one man in a crowd with so many needs attract such focused attention from Jesus? I said earlier that Israel's thirty-eight years in the wilderness was an opening act to this miracle at the Pool of Bethesda. This intentional walk toward one man was planned. Let's keep reading to find out why.

> Now a certain man was there who had an infirmity thirty-eight years. When Jesus saw him lying there, and knew that he already had been in that condition a long time, He said to him, "Do you want to be made well?"
>
> The sick man answered Him, "Sir, I have no man to put me into the pool when the water is stirred up; but while I am coming, another steps down before me." Jesus said to him, "Rise, take up your bed and walk." And immediately the man was made well, took up his bed, and walked. And that day was the Sabbath. (vv. 5–9)

This man had been bedridden in that awful revolving door of pain for thirty-eight years. How did he survive all those years? Who took care of him and fed him? Who cleaned his bedsores? Who emptied his bedpan? Perhaps another invalid who wasn't as bad off begged for a few morsels of bread and a few shekels each day and helped him. Perhaps he had a son or daughter living nearby who checked on him during the long days and weeks, year after year, as people around him disappeared into their graves.

I've visited the Pool of Bethesda and imagined what it might have looked like on the day Jesus came through the nearby Sheep Gate. The scene of so many burdened souls hoping against hope for the moving of the water—surely the atmosphere would have been heavy with despair.

Years before I stood at the Pool of Bethesda, I was invited to meet Mother Teresa at her convent, the Missionaries of Charity, in Calcutta, India. After our half-hour meeting, I was taken to

Mother Teresa's Home for the Destitute and Dying. There, in a building no larger than a medium-sized house, lay hundreds of dying Hindus. Their religion taught them that if they had the unfortunate fate of being born into a lower caste there was no way out for them. Only poverty and sickness awaited them in life. You could smell disease. You could hear their death rattles, that sound lungs make gasping for a fleeting breath. You could see the faces—actually no faces at all—eaten away by leprosy. All the nuns and volunteers could do was to fill the dying with morphine and help them pass with some semblance of dignity. I can tell you I have never witnessed such horror before or since.

However, I don't remember the sights and smells of that place as much as I do the wave after wave of self-pity in all its mocking triumph. These people had been taught that accepting their fate might lead to the possibility of reincarnation into a higher caste. As a result, they learned to glory in the impossibility of any sliver or ray of hope shining into their miserable world. They had become feeble pacifists and dared not shake their fists in one final protest at fatalism's lie. On that day I saw firsthand where self-pity would lead me should I ever give in to its ruse. I wanted no part of it, then or now. When I closed my eyes at the Pool of Bethesda it wasn't hard to imagine the kind of scene Jesus witnessed.

Think of history, and that moment at the pool that day, coming together. Israel had spent thirty-eight years wandering in self-pity in the wilderness, feeling like victims. They were in sight of the Promised Land but couldn't get in. They were dependent on someone else feeding them. Israel's thirty-eight years of misery finally came to an end with an announcement from God: "Now rise and cross over" (Deut. 2:13).

When Jesus comes to Bethesda, He picks out a man who had wandered in a wilderness of self-pity for thirty-eight years, feeling like a victim. The man was in sight of a pool filled with promise but couldn't get in. He was dependent on someone else feeding him. And his thirty-eight years of misery finally came to an end with an announcement from God: "Rise, take up your bed and walk" (John 5:8).

I've sometimes been puzzled by the question Jesus asked the sick man: "Do you want to be made well?" The answer seems obvious, so why would Jesus ask such a question? But when you read the question in context it's clear. "When Jesus saw him lying there, and knew that he had been in that condition a long time, He said to him, 'do you want to be made well?'" (v. 6). Jesus knew when a person is bound by self-pity for a long season they grow used to it and sometimes would rather just stay in that condition. The man's answer shows us that Jesus knew what He was asking and why He asked it: "The sick man answered Him, 'Sir, I have no man to put me into the pool when the water is stirred up; but while I am coming, another steps down before me'" (v. 7). Translation: "No one cares about me and I have no hope of ever being healed." Thirty-eight years of self-pity had left the man bound in unbelief.

I've also wondered why Jesus told the sick man to take up his bed on his way out of that place. The mat he had been lying on for so long wouldn't have been the most sanitary thing in the world. Why would Jesus want him to pick it up and take it with him? There are two possibilities. First, I would assume that after all those years the man likely had preferred seating at the Pool of Bethesda. His bed was probably on the edge of the water. He had a coveted place and perhaps a bit of seniority and respect because of the longevity of his stay. Not enough respect, of course, for others to help him into the pool when the waters were stirred. When people are hungry and sick and desperate, it's not uncommon for them to exhibit the instincts of wounded animals. So, for this man, after years of being passed over, his place in line may have become the only dignity he had left. When self-pity actually becomes dignity, our pathway to resilience has been severely roadblocked. By taking up his bed he would have been giving up his place of honor in order to choose a better life.

Jesus knew walking away from this place of self-pity was a required act of faith that would bring a miracle. The allure of self-pity is so powerful that many choose to stay in the security of their familiar surroundings even if they're miserable. Someone once said, "A familiar captivity is frequently more desirable than an unfamiliar freedom," and I think that's a good point.

The second reason why I think Jesus told him to take up his bed is because it was a Sabbath, and Jesus knew the religious authorities would immediately challenge the man for carrying his bed on a Sabbath day, which they did. "The Jews therefore said to him who was cured, 'It is the Sabbath; it is not lawful for you to carry your bed'" (v. 10). Jesus knew that a direct challenge to the man's resolve to walk away from thirty-eight years of self-pity would actually help him break free from its grasp.

Self-pity says, "Get back into your hole. Lay that bed back down where you picked it up. You're too wounded to carry such a load. You're not strong enough. Don't you know you're paralyzed? Lie back down and let me comfort you just a little while longer until you get your strength up." Jesus says, "Rise, take up your bed, and get out of this place because thirty-eight years is long enough!"

What message was Jesus sending to Israel by singling out this man for healing? The man's sickness had worn down his resolve to the point where he had become paralyzed by self-pity and unbelief. His thirty-eight years of physical, spiritual, and emotional stagnation represented Israel's thirty-eight years of stagnation in their wilderness wanderings. Jesus was sending a clear message to the Jewish people that they were again trapped in a place of self-pity and unbelief. The healing of this man, Jesus's first major public miracle, was a sign to Israel that God's mercy could once again bring them out of their bondage and despair.

There Is a Way Out

But what does this miracle mean to us? It means Jesus is concerned about people who are trapped in the revolving door of self-pity. It means He intentionally seeks out people whose pain and hurt and loss have worn them down to the point where they haven't the strength to help themselves. It means Jesus specifically looks for people in crowded hellholes who have run out of options and whose friends have grown weary of tending to their wounds. It means Jesus has mercy (remember, Bethesda means "house of mercy") for the soul bound by self-pity. It means Jesus can find you wherever you are, no matter how far you have sunk in despair. It means that if you fasten your faith to Jesus's "take up your bed and walk," you can break the spell self-pity has over you no matter if your resilience has been blocked for thirty-eight minutes or thirty-eight years.

Think of this: the miracle at the Pool of Bethesda would have never been recorded in the Bible if the sick man refused to rise up and out of his despair. This means removing the first roadblock to resilience—self-pity—is going to require bold faith on your part. The man's thirty-eight years of suffering opened the door for him to be the recipient of Jesus's first major public miracle. His story has been recorded in the pages of the Bible and told all over the earth.

■ ■ ■

The old-world sensibility of the rule keepers at the Royal Calcutta Golf Club offers us a great lesson in life today. Play the ball where the monkey dropped it. Press on regardless. Never allow a seemingly impossible problem to paralyze your progress with self-pity. The man at the Pool of Bethesda teaches us a great lesson as well. No matter how long you've been paralyzed by self-pity, there is a way out for you. The pain of your past does not have to rule your future. The pain of your past can actually be the canvas of your future masterpiece. Your story of resilience may one day be told around the world!

BOUNCE TAKEAWAY:
Reflect on Your Own Story

1. If you are suffering from self-pity, what life circumstance allowed this sinister roadblock to gain entrance into your heart? (Think about this question for a few minutes, because the roadblock of self-pity may have entrapped you earlier than you think.)

2. Here is a tough question: How much time do you give self-pity each day to soothe and comfort you in order to avoid the pain you must pass through to achieve a comeback?

3. Here is a way to determine if you're going to overcome the roadblock of self-pity: On a scale of 1–10 (10 being the highest), what is the level of your desire to bounce back? If it's 9 or less, you are allowing self-pity to undermine your path toward resilience.

BOUNCE CHALLENGE #5

In your bounce journal, write:

In my life I have either reasons or results. Today I have decided to overcome all the reasons I can't rise out of my heartache and setbacks. I reject all feelings of self-pity that first came into my life when . . . (describe the moment and circumstances when self-pity first entered into your heart).

Now I encourage you to pray this prayer of deliverance from self-pity and break its hold on your mind:

In the name of Jesus Christ I renounce the root and the fruit of self-pity that has thrown up a roadblock to my resilience. I desire to be healed and restored and to recover fully and completely. Today in Jesus's name I take up my bed and walk, and I proclaim I will never come back to this horrible place of self-pity again! I renounce all of the emotional attachments I have with the comforting and soothing voice of self-pity and I rise up today out of the despair the deception of self-pity has brought into my life. Amen!

6

Disappointment

A Friend Named Mike

The world breaks every one and afterward many are
strong at the broken places.

Ernest Hemingway, *A Farewell to Arms*

Scary movies are a multimillion-dollar business in Hollywood. Maybe we just need to watch others battle zombies to gain courage for our own struggles. But I've learned a lot about disappointment from observation of another kind: the uncommon blessing of watching godly people handle their heartaches. And the person who has taught me the most about responding to unexpected disappointments—those gut-wrenching painful surprises I never dreamed I'd have to endure—is my friend Mike Coleman.

What made it possible for Mike to teach me? Learning from each other is part of why God gave us the church. When we come together as the body of Christ, we have the opportunity to form lasting friendships with individuals who are suffering and experience mutual encouragement. We connect and then share our stories, and in the process we pull each other up out of the pit. Proverbs tell us, "A friend loves at all times, and a brother is born for adversity," and again, "As iron sharpens iron, so a man sharpens the countenance of his friend" (Prov. 17:17; 27:17). The wisdom of going through trials with a brother or sister at your side is reinforced in Ecclesiastes 4:9–10: "Two are better than one, because they have a good reward for their labor. For if they fall, one will lift up his companion. But woe to him who is alone when he falls, for he has no one to help him up."

In the introduction to his translation of the book of Job, Eugene Peterson says, "We need to quit feeling sorry for people who suffer and instead look up to them, learn from them, and—if they will let us—join them in protest and prayer. Pity can be nearsighted and condescending."[1] It is vital, when you are dealing with heartache, to find someone you can learn from and they from you. How do you find those kind of friends? Someone once told me that to have a friend you must be a friend. Covenant friendships, those friendships based on a shared bond to seek God's highest and best for each other, take years to develop, but the benefit of fellowship and accountability is immeasurable.

Mike is one of those friends. He was the CEO of Integrity Media for twenty-five years and also its cofounder. Integrity's mission statement was "Helping people worldwide experience the manifest presence of God." The main bread and butter of the company was worship music, and millions of lives (including my own) were touched by the songs of praise they distributed. The company's worldwide vision of helping people experience the presence of God spread like a canopy over the globe, and Integrity music and media products were distributed in more than 160 nations.

And then the unexpected happened. New technology exploded onto the world scene that opened the door to illegal digital downloading of music. This had a devastating financial effect on the entire music industry, both Christian and secular. It's hard to compete against free.

In 2011 Mike sold the company after years of declining sales and walked away from a life vision that had filled his heart for twenty-five years. Disappointing? Of course. But being a resilient person, Mike began to lay plans for another chapter in his life and a new season of ministry.

But again something disappointing and unexpected happened. Mike got sick. In fact, Mike got really sick. In October 2012, Mike underwent major spine surgery in his neck. After several other health complications were added to the scenario, Mike was weakened to the point where he had a difficult time driving or even walking across a room. His plans for a new season of ministry were shelved. For the next few years, at least, Mike would be physically disabled and unable to work.

How do you respond when your life vision vanishes before your eyes? What do you do when you find yourself at the crossroads of expectation and disappointment? What are you to think? Where do you go from there? How do you recover from something like that?

Mike and I connected in 2012. Maybe our friendship started because we were both in a place of adversity. Today I cherish Mike as a brother who was born to help me through my adversity, and I believe I was born to help him through his. I have learned priceless truths from Mike's life. The uncanny thing is that in the five years I've been walking with him in friendship, I have never heard him express doubt in God's love for him or bitterness about his circumstances. Rather, he is what I would call a model of extreme resilience. Here are two truths Mike has taught me that have challenged my perspective of disappointment.

First of all, Mike once told me, "Life is more defined by the unexpected than by the expected." In other words, your character is not shaped by how you face the expected things in life but by how you face those unexpected things at the crossroads where your expectation meets disappointment. You see, you expect it to be cold in the winter so you handle it. A woman expects pain in childbirth so it helps her endure. You expect the tires on your car to wear with age, wrinkles to form on your face as you grow older, your stomach to growl when you're hungry, and your taxes to be due on April 15. Living through these expected things doesn't really define you. You are defined instead by how you respond to the unexpected events in your life: a stillborn baby, a sudden and tragic loss of a loved one, the loss of a business, a divorce, a child who develops an incurable disease. How we handle the unexpected is really what defines us.

Mike also gave me another golden principle that has changed my understanding of disappointment. He once said to me, "Aaron, it says in Romans 8:28, 'And we know that all things work together for good to those who love God.'" Then he asked, "How do you define *good*?" My definition was shallow and, quite frankly, pathetic: "All things working together for good means that God takes all the things I'm going through—all of my pain and loss—and He works them out and in the end He gives me my life back and my things back and I'm back up on top of the world again. That's good."

Mike responded by saying, "Aaron, I think there is something even better than that. I think the definition of *good* is when you come through the pain of disappointment and joyfully discover you have been shaped a little more into the nature and character of Jesus, to the point where you are so content and fulfilled with what God has done in you that getting your treasure back is no longer a major concern. In the end, the real treasure is Jesus."

I believe Mike is right: this is what *good* ultimately is. Today, Mike continues the steady climb out of his crucible and is experiencing healing and fresh vision. He now serves as the CEO of a new ministry that utilizes the power of media to reframe the state of Israel and the Jewish people in a positive light in the face of global anti-Semitism.

We all have our disappointments in life and we can't rate our pain of disappointment by someone else's, nor would we want to. I don't find solace for my wounds in the unfortunate tragedy of another. The reason, of course, is that the feeling of disappointment is real—it simply doesn't make you feel any better to compare your disappointments to Mike's. "Oh, I feel so much better about my agony now that I've heard Mike's story." It just doesn't work that way. So why do I share his story? It is not because of the nature of his heartache but because of how he responded to it. That's the story.

What I want to know is how Mike came out of this. How did he write a new chapter? In every great story there are always four elements: the setting, the conflict, the climax, and the resolution. After the sale of Mike's company and the loss of his health, did his story continue? Did he ever become strong at the broken places? Did he ever find a resolution to his heartbreak? Did he make peace with his pain?

My brother-in-law Stu wrote a tagline for his public relations company: "Because our stories become us." That's an apt description of human endeavor. For Mike, his season of difficulty was either going to become his story, the thing people remembered about him, the stuff from which he would never recover, or the beginning of a comeback. It would be the end—or the beginning.

In the last chapter, we learned how self-pity leads to disappointment, disappointment leads to resentment, and resentment leads to indecisiveness. It's important to know these roadblocks work progressively. Allow self-pity to take root and disappointment is sure to follow. You may be affected by disappointment more than you think.

You Will Never Be "Dissed" from a Divine Appointment

Not only can disappointment take root in our souls because of losses like Mike endured but it can also take up residence when things don't work out the way we planned. You might say disappointment is an appointment that never happened as expected, a dissed-appointment. However disappointment comes your way, it can leave you with feelings of abandonment and vulnerability.

Often, we blame our disappointments on God: "God, why didn't You prevent the accident from happening? Where were You when I needed You? Are You concerned about me? Are You fair? Are You aware of what I'm going through?" We can pick up this sentiment in Martha's disappointment in Christ for not coming sooner to the bedside of her dying brother, Lazarus: "Lord, if You had been here, my brother would not have died" (John 11:21).

It's convenient for us finite humans to connect our disappointments to God's infinite character. I mean, someone has to be responsible around here, don't they? We passionately will things into being, thinking we're like Jim Carey's character, Bruce, in the film *Bruce Almighty*. We will into existence the American dream and a Disneyland life. Should we suddenly be awakened by the annoying alarm clock of adversity, we wonder why God didn't create a snooze button so we could dream right through recessions, bankruptcies, splintering family conflicts, real estate short sales, and missed quotas.

Maybe we have created a god in our minds that is not God at all. A kind of great wizard behind a curtain who responds to all of our wishes and wants and keeps disappointment from even getting close to the security fence he's erected around our lives. That's some kind of god.

You Have a Date with Destiny

Each person who follows Christ has a divine assignment in life. Some call it a divine appointment. A friend of mine tells a story from his high school years about a girl he was secretly infatuated with. Her name was Destiny. He was love struck, and when she finally agreed to go out with him he enthusiastically announced, "Tonight, I have a date with Destiny!" This is true for Christians. Each of us has a date with destiny. Jesus confirms this in John's Gospel: "You did not choose Me, but I chose you and appointed you that you should go and bear fruit" (15:16). Each believer in Jesus has been chosen and appointed. The opposite of appointment is dis-appointment. However, Christ never dis-appoints people. He appoints and then re-appoints if we should ever miss a divine appointment, but He never dis-appoints us from our purpose. Could it be that disappointments often come our way because we make appointments with God He never agreed to? That's like sitting in a doctor's waiting room growing all the more discouraged when the nurse doesn't call your name—only to realize at the end of the day that you never scheduled an appointment.

Could it be that disappointment is actually a grace? How can this be? When I am disappointed in my circumstances or in other people, the pain of that moment leads me to trust the only One who can truly satisfy the longings and dreams in my soul. And with that trust arises faith. And when my faith brings me to the place where I believe no matter what my situation that God's love for me is perfect and His wisdom is infallible, my disappointment fades away. The Scriptures affirm this: "Whoever believes in Him will not be disappointed" (Rom. 10:11 NASB).

The agenda of disappointment is to slowly and systematically deteriorate your faith and ultimately introduce you to resentment and indecisiveness. That's why this roadblock to your resilience must be exposed. Like self-pity, disappointment works subtly, and you may not even notice it lulling you to sleep. Its insidiousness is like an invisible gas. Coal miners knew the dangers of something so quietly dangerous as methane gas. They would take a canary with them into the mine. If the canary was singing, all was well. But if the canary seemed drowsy, dazed, or worse, the miners made a quick exit to the fresh air of the outside world, escaping certain death.

Hashtag: People Will Disappoint You

Here's a headline for you: people are human and prone to failure. My own life was broken by someone's selfish choice. A drunk driver took the life of my father when I was three years old. For years I questioned God and tried to understand why I had to grow up without a dad. The roadblock of self-pity was taking root in my heart, and its companions—disappointment, resentment, and indecisiveness—were sure to follow. Thankfully, I came to terms with the fact that my father was killed by a drunk driver because a flawed human being made a series of really unfortunate decisions.

We cannot change the reality that everyone around us, at one point or another, is going to disappoint us. Especially those we love the most. We are all part of the human family with all of its deficiencies. If we cannot accept human weakness and the propensity of others to disappoint us, often for unexplainable reasons, we will eventually crumble. You just can't go on believing you, of all people, are somehow immune from the sickness spread by broken people.

Our refusal to accept disappointment in our relationships causes us to suffer unnecessary agony, like an aching sore neck or a twisted back that even a hot bath in Epsom salts can't relieve. We simply cannot expect divinity from humanity. As a younger man, I let the failures of people in my life become roadblocks to God's plans for me. I lay awake literally hundreds of nights pondering the odd decisions and motivations of others. *How could they do something so strange?* And do you know what I learned after these years of sleepless nights? One thing: I will never understand why people do what they do. Now that I'm older and wiser, I no longer experience sleepless nights of trying to contemplate others' behaviors. I now accept the fact that other people are imperfect creatures just like me. I accept that those around me will unintentionally—and sometimes, yes, intentionally—disappointment me. And I'm okay with that.

The Discipline of Disillusionment

In his book *My Utmost for His Highest*, Oswald Chambers encourages us to see people as they really are: imperfect and fallible. In his devotional for July 30, entitled "The Discipline of Disillusionment," Chambers opens with John 2:24–25: "Jesus did not commit himself unto them . . . for he knew what was in man" (KJV). And then he unveils an amazing commentary about the discipline required to keep us from being disillusioned and disappointed in others.

Chambers urges us to drop our illusions, our desire to make others the perfect cushion to all our falls and the salve to all our wounds. He says that we need to take our focus off others and instead look to our Lord as the only One who can be perfect. Imagine how much more you might love your spouse or coworkers if you stopped expecting perfection from them. He calls this realization a grace! Once you learn to seek Jesus alone, and realize that others aren't the be-all and end-all, you will bypass the disappointment roadblock.

Two Reactions to Disappointment

I have found there are two reactions to disappointment when it makes its grand entrance into our world. The first response we have is to believe disappointment is the result of a lack of faith. This denies the fact that, in this life, disappointments are going to come. We can muster up all of the faith in the world and disappointment will still knock on our door from time to time. Our faith does not prevent disappointment; it carries us through the valley of grief that disappointment carves. The idea that disappointment is caused by a lack of faith misses the grace it really is. The writer of Ecclesiastes eloquently portrays this: "In the day of prosperity be joyful, but in the day of adversity consider: Surely God has appointed the one as well as the other" (Eccles. 7:14).

The second response when disappointment comes calling is fundamentally fatalistic. It's the belief that disappointment is always lurking in the shadows, ready to hit the kill switch. So we think the best approach to life is to lower our expectations and faith. The motto for this way of thinking is found in this nugget from seventeenth-century poet Alexander Pope: "Blessed is the man who expects nothing, for he shall never be disappointed."

But why can't there be a balance? Why can't we just live in high hope, great faith, and expectation about our future and at the same time believe that, should disappointment come our way, it's just an expected part of doing something new? Could this be the place where we meet God and understand Him for who He really is, not who we have created Him to be?

Yes, at this intersection of disappointment and expectation I bring my disappointments to God, trusting in Him to help me make sense of the chaos. If I don't share my disappointments with God, I'm actually neglecting His desire to heal and transform me and get me moving again. Mike Coleman's life expectations got hammered when the worldwide music industry was changed by technology. It was in that place, where his expectation suffered the wounds of disappointment, that he would eventually see his reflection in the face of God and find the deeper purpose of his painful journey.

Meeting God at the Intersection of Disappointment and Expectation

One of the great biblical examples of finding God at the intersection of disappointment and expectation is the story of John the

Baptist. John had labored for years paving the way for Jesus's ministry. He lived in the hot and arid desert, clothing himself in camel hair and existing on a diet of locusts dipped in wild honey. Not exactly a life of luxury for the man given two world-changing tasks: calling Israel to a baptism of repentance and preparing Israel to receive the Messiah.

When Jesus came on the scene, John declared, "He must increase, but I must decrease" (John 3:30). All of John's messianic expectations were in Jesus. The hope of John, and all of Israel for that matter, was that the Messiah would usher in a glorious earthly kingdom, and for this reason, those years spent in the wilderness were meaningful and purposeful. John stepped down from the limelight of ministry to serve the greater purpose of Jesus establishing His kingdom. John must have felt an extreme sense of gratification and thankfulness seeing Jesus's ministry expand and grow, knowing the kingdom of God was soon to burst upon the world scene in an epiphany of glorious light.

But disappointment set in when Jesus seemed to be doing more teaching, preaching, and healing than kingdom building. Something about Jesus's message and mission didn't sit well with John the Baptist. By now, he thought, Jesus should be doing something much more significant than opening blind eyes and preaching to the poor. Wresting political power from the Roman Empire would be a good start, but that didn't seem to be on Jesus's ministry agenda.

In the meantime, John was thrown into prison because he confronted King Herod for sleeping with the king's sister-in-law. Rotting in a jail cell awaiting an uncertain fate, John began to doubt Jesus's credibility. It's a wonder that such disappointment could take root in a man like John, especially after witnessing the supernatural when he baptized Jesus in the Jordon River: "And the Holy Spirit descended in bodily form like a dove upon Him, and a voice came from heaven which said, 'You are My beloved Son; in You I am well pleased'" (Luke 3:22).

This says to me that no one is immune from the temptation of disappointment. With his expectations in ruins, John confronted Jesus with an unthinkable question: "Now when John, while imprisoned, heard of the works of Christ, he sent word by his disciples and said to Him, 'Are You the Expected One, or shall we look for someone else?'" (Matt. 11:2–3 NASB).

What an amazing question. John is normally not held in high esteem for the audacity of his inquiry. Some may be persuaded to think, *How dare he ask Jesus such a ridiculous question! Doesn't he know who he's talking to? This is the Lamb of God, announced by the Father's voice from heaven and confirmed by the Holy Spirit resting on Him.*

But I, for one, really appreciate John's question, because it lets me know he knew something about the nature of Jesus I tend to forget. John knew he could be a broken human being in God's presence and not receive forty lashes. He knew he could be real, vulnerable, and expressive, sharing his disappointments and brokenhearted questions without being rebuked or told to just suck it up. Maybe, more than a question, it was a plea for help and clarity coming from a friend wasting away in a gloomy dungeon. "Are you the Expected One or should we look for someone else?" I think John had the pressing intuition that Herod was going to kill him (which Herod later did) and so he wanted to have one last conversation with his friend Jesus. When I read this question, I realize John is meeting Jesus at the crossroads of expectation and disappointment. I think John in his human frailty and weakness needed an encouraging word from the Lord to not give up on his faith and hope in the messianic promise.

What's so intriguing about this exchange between the Baptist and the Christ was not the question but the answer. Jesus didn't rebuff John or speak harshly to him, thinking it an insult to be asked such a thing. Instead, Jesus lovingly replied to John's disciples, "Go and tell John the things which you hear and see.

The blind see and the lame walk; the lepers are cleansed and the deaf hear; the dead are raised up and the poor have the gospel preached to them. And blessed is he who is not offended because of Me" (vv. 4–6).

What is so amazing about Jesus's reply is that all of the things He listed about His ministry were Old Testament predictions of what the Messiah would one day accomplish. In listing these signs Jesus was saying, "John, I know I've blown your expectations but let Me give you a piece of information you may not have considered. You have assumed I would initially come as a conquering King, but according to Scripture, the Messiah will first come as a healer. John, I will fulfill all of the Scriptures concerning who I am but you'll just have to be patient. In the meantime, friend, don't allow the roadblocks of self-pity and disappointment to grow into resentment toward Me." What a reassuring answer! What a friend! Right in the middle of the intersection of disappointment and expectation, John the Baptist brings his painful question to Jesus: "Are You the Expected One or should we look for someone else?" And instead of rejecting him, Jesus assures him that He is indeed the One he prepared the way for.

We Raise Ourselves toward God by the Questions We Ask Him

In the book *Night*, a vivid recollection about surviving the horrors of the Holocaust, author Elie Wiesel relates the dialogue he had with Moishe, a leader from a Jewish Orthodox house of prayer:

> He had watched me one day as I prayed at dusk. "Why do you cry when you pray?" he asked, as though he knew me well. "I don't know," I answered, troubled. I had never asked myself that question. I cried because . . . because something inside me felt the need to cry. That was all I knew. "Why do you pray?" Strange question. Why did I live? Why did I breathe? "I don't know," I

told him, even more troubled and ill at ease. "I don't know." From that day on, I saw him often. He explained to me, with great emphasis, that every question possessed a power that was lost in the answer. . . . Man comes closer to God through the questions he asks Him, he liked to say. Therein lies true dialogue. Man asks and God replies. . . . "And why do you pray, Moishe?" I asked him. "I pray to the God within me for the strength to ask Him the real questions."[2]

In the New Testament, people asked Jesus lots of questions and He answered all of them—except a handful asked by religious leaders attempting to trap Him by His words. This says to me Jesus isn't offended by requests for clarity when disappointment comes and expectations are ruined. God longs to dialogue with us, especially in our despair.

When Mary the sister of Lazarus was in the midst of grief over her brother's death, she approached Jesus and said, "If You had been here, my brother would not have died" (John 11:32). She was really saying, "Where were You when we needed You? You could have prevented this and You didn't. Why?" And what was Jesus's reaction? Was He angry or offended? Not even close. Jesus responded to Mary with one of the most tender questions in the Bible: "Where have you laid him?" (v. 34).

Jesus so loves you He is unwilling to allow you to go on living with buried dreams and hopes. He is constantly attempting to draw you back to the intersection where your expectations were crushed by disappointment and help you find meaning in the night season. In Jesus's conversation with Mary's sister Martha, He asked her if she believed He was the resurrection and the life. That's the ultimate question for all of us, isn't it? Do we believe Jesus can resurrect long-dead expectations and leave behind an empty tomb once filled with the grave clothes of disappointment? Ask Lazarus that question, because he left that tomb.

To Mary Magdalene, who was disappointed upon finding the tomb empty, believing someone had taken Jesus's body away, He asked, "Woman, why are you weeping?" (20:15). To Peter, who was disappointed in himself for denying the Lord three times, Jesus asked, "Simon, son of Jonah, do you love Me?" (21:16). With the question came an assignment that encouraged Peter to move past his disappointment: "Tend My sheep" (v. 16). Jesus was empathetic toward Peter in his brokenness and restored him to his place of ministry after a disappointing failure.

Then there were the two men on the road to Emmaus, their expectations crushed at the news of Jesus's crucifixion because they "were hoping that it was He who was going to redeem Israel" (Luke 24:21). As they walked and talked along the road leading them out of Jerusalem, three days after Jesus's death, a mysterious man joined them. The Scriptures say they were kept from recognizing that the man was Jesus, there at the crossroads of disappointment and expectation. The crucifixion battered and broke Jesus beyond recognition, and I believe He still bore those marks even after His resurrection. I wonder, too, if it wasn't their own disappointment that made it impossible for them to see Him. Have you ever had that experience? The truth, a way out of your disappointment and self-pity, might be right in front of you, walking right next to you, and since you can't even imagine that God is there offering you a way out, you simply can't see Him. So these two tired, dusty Jewish travelers, their heads hanging low, tell the man walking with them about everything that's happened, even how the women and the other disciples had gone to the tomb on two occasions and reported the same thing: the tomb was empty. But did that give them hope? No! They were so deep in the gutter of their disappointment they couldn't even see over the curb.

Jesus said to them, after they tell their tale of woe, "Oh foolish ones, and slow of heart to believe in all that the prophets have spoken! Ought not the Christ to have suffered these things and to enter into His glory?" (vv. 25–26). This was a piece of information they had not considered.

When they reached the village where they were staying, they asked Jesus to join them for the evening. As they sat at the table, Jesus took bread and broke it and served it to them. Immediately their eyes were opened and Jesus disappeared from their sight. And then, the "Duh!" moment: "And they said to one another, 'Did not our heart burn within us while He talked with us on the road, and while He opened the Scriptures to us?" (v. 32). When they finally looked up out of their grief and into the possibility that everything the prophets foretold might be true, they finally saw Jesus. It dissolved their disappointments and inspired fresh expectation. In joy they rushed back to Jerusalem to tell the eleven disciples. "And they told about the things that had happened on the road, and how He was known to them in the breaking of bread" (v. 35).

It's in that same place that Jesus is known to us, in the breaking of the bread—those places where we are being pulled apart like a loaf of bread. Those places where everyone wants a piece of us and we've got nothing left to give. Jesus comes to us in those painful intersections where our expectations have been crushed by disappointment and is known to us in our most vulnerable moments of brokenness.

The Rest of Mike's Story

As I'm writing these words, my friend Mike Coleman is preparing for a comeback. You could say the pain of disappointment he's endured the last five years is the introduction to the next season of his life, where all the pages are still blank because the story hasn't been written yet. And when he comes out he's going to have one great story to tell of God's faithfulness toward him in the furnace of affliction. In the meantime, Mike continues to embrace his present situation with a joy that's void of overwhelming feelings of disappointment. That's a testimony of God's grace.

If you have been broken by disappointing circumstances, remember what Mike told me: "We are not defined by how we handle the expected events in our lives but by the unexpected." If your expectations have been dashed on the rocks of disappointment, there's a silver lining in the experience—even though the stitching part stings. As you embrace this time of unexpected disappointment you are being defined, sharpened, and shaped into the nature of the One who called you—Jesus. You may not see it now, but one day your scars of disappointment will define the bedrock of who you really are.

BOUNCE TAKEAWAY:
Reflect on Your Own Story

1. Have you ever considered that disappointment is a grace? Look back over your life and think about those times when your expectations met disappointment at the crossroads. How did the disappointing thing actually turn out to be a grace?

2. Have you ever (like me) lost sleep over trying to figure out why people disappoint you? What are you learning about the imperfection of our human nature when it comes to our ability to disappoint one another? Are you coming to accept the reality that people will disappoint you? (The answer to this question is liberating.)

3. Have you ever considered that God welcomes your questions about your disappointments? Have you ever freely expressed your disappointments to Him? If not, what is the reason for your silence?

BOUNCE CHALLENGE #6

Do you have a disappointment you are struggling with and trying to find the reason behind? I encourage you to bring your disappointing heartaches to God. If you are at the crossroads where expectation has met a disappointing loss, please pray this prayer with me:

> *Father God, I bring to You today my disappointment* (right here I want you to write down in your bounce journal exactly what your disappointment is, and then continue on in the prayer). *I don't know why this is happening and I'm struggling right now. I really desire to know not necessarily why this happened but what You want me to learn in the process. If there is something I'm missing—a piece of information that will give me Your divine perspective about this moment in my life—my ears and heart are open to hear Your still small voice.*

Here is your challenge: dare to share your disappointments with God. Read Psalm 34 and Psalm 138:3, 8. Meditate on these passages of Scripture that describe King David's confidence that God desires to dialogue with His children. After you have read the Word, begin to express your heartache to your heavenly Father. Now, take time to listen to God's still small voice as He answers you. I am confident you will hear Him speak fresh wisdom and clarity into your spirit about the matters that concern you. As God begins to clarify things to you, I encourage you to write them down in this section of your bounce journal.

7

Resentment toward God

For God's Sake, Where Is God?

I have not lost faith in God. I have moments of anger
and protest. Sometimes I've been closer to Him for
that reason.

Elie Wiesel, *New York Times*, Oct. 15, 1986

It was reported by German SS guards stationed in the death
camps during the Holocaust that they often heard singing coming from the gas chambers. And what was the song the Jewish men,
women, and children sang as the diesel engines began to cough
and spurt out dizzying and stomach-turning fumes, carburetors
choking from the ashes of the crematorium ovens in a kind of
low, guttural, pulsating rhythm that almost sounded like a voice
muttering something about the grave, and pumping Zyklon B gas

into innocent lungs? The song they sang was inspired by Deuteronomy 6, and it is known as the Shema:

> Hear, Israel, the Lord is our God, the Lord is One.
> Blessed be the Name of His glorious kingdom for ever and
>   ever.
> And you shall love the Lord your God with all your heart
>   and with all your soul and with all your might.

Remarkably, these Jewish martyrs, systematically hunted down
by the Nazis in every fissure and crack and ghetto in Europe, their
gaunt and dehydrated bodies crammed and pressed by strong Aryan
backs into cattle cars with no ventilation or light, carried to certain
death solely because they were God's chosen people, whispered
out their final breaths to laud this same God as worthy of their
total love and devotion. This is heart-wrenching. You would think
their voices would have been lifted in defiance and protest toward
the God of heaven. Instead, they sang Him an anthem of praise.

This same phenomenon of devotion was found in the Gestapo
prison in Cologne, Germany. The cells in the belly of this behe-
moth were built to house two inmates each, but the German high
command was fixated on a frenetic killing spree and required more
victims waiting in the wings. So the Germans forced thirty people
into each nine-by-nine-foot space. On the bitterly cold stone walls
of these cells, over 1,800 graffiti scrawls have been left behind,
many of which are messages of affection, even instructions to
family members, a kind of primitive last will and testament, such
as, "You will grow up and be big, and support your mother in her
old age, steering the car with a steady hand, flying over the beloved
country's expanses. Don't forget, remember, look at your father's
photograph."[1] One of the most poignant is this poem:

> I believe in the sun
> even when it is not shining.

And I believe in love,
even when there's no one there.
And I believe in God,
even when he is silent.[2]

In the book *The Holocaust: Where Was God?* Art Katz writes:

The Holocaust is the indigestible lump and the most significant factor of modern Jewish life on account of the magnitude of what took place. It is the single most devastating event of modern times, not just for the Jew, but for the whole of the modern world. There has not been any event in recent history that has prompted more writing, more research, and more literature. . . . But there is very little literature at all on the question of, "Where was God and why did He allow it?" . . . Among the things the Holocaust reveals is that we have naively and idealistically subscribed to traditional notions about God. Those inadequate notions have created in us a tremendous emotional, mental, and spiritual upheaval. To our way of thinking, when the "God" we subscribe to should have revealed Himself as God in power and in ability to intervene, He was silent. It raises the question of either a God who has a moral defect of indifference to suffering, particularly of His own people, or a God who is powerless to effect any change, or simply a God who is not.[3]

When God Is Silent

The Holocaust created a moral dilemma for all of us. If we are charged by God with a moral mandate to show empathy to the afflicted, should not the One who set the standard, at just the bare minimum, be present and accounted for when people suffer, especially His own chosen people? This dilemma has become a stumbling block and caused resentment toward God for Jewish people the world over. Their argument is, "How can God portray Himself as a God of lovingkindness and yet when our people were viciously and bestially slaughtered, He did nothing? We proclaimed

His name with our last breaths in the gas chambers and ovens of Auschwitz-Birkenau, Dachau, Bergen-Belsen, Treblinka . . . and He remained silent."

As a result of the Holocaust, many Jews conclude God is sadistic rather than compassionate and they want no part of Him. I am Jewish by birth and I've traveled many times to Israel to visit my family. Our conversations always migrate to the Shoah (the Holocaust) and the moral dilemma about God encountered there. It may come as a surprise to you, but the majority of Israeli Jews are atheists because of their resentment at the silence of God during the genocide of His own people.

The issue of God's silence in suffering can become a roadblock for all of us. It's in those times when the hurt is on and you breathe a prayer—sometimes many prayers—calling on His name, extolling His lovingkindness toward you, crying out in quiet desperation for some relief, from the One who has promised intervention in your time of need, and the heavens answer not a word. It's in those times you may feel like raising a fist toward the sky and shouting, "Where are You, God?!"

I think we're sometimes like Mary and her sister Martha who, when caring for their sick brother Lazarus, petitioned Jesus with the words, "Lord, behold, he whom You love is sick" (John 11:3). They were reminding Him this was not just some ordinary casual acquaintance but a close friend. They were saying, "Jesus, You've healed a lot of people You don't even know, and if You would do that for them, surely You would respond immediately to the 'one You love.'"

This family had been hospitable to Jesus. He had eaten at their table and stayed in their home; in other words, they did life together. Their petition was filled with the assurance of His love for them: "the one You love is sick." They were certain He would not forget them nor refuse their request but come to their aid—immediately— because He loved them. And yet Jesus remained silent and Lazarus died. Why? Jesus allowed His friend to die so He could raise him from the dead, and in the end God was glorified by the miracle.

Though hard to understand, God's answers are often found in His silence. As Jesus writhed in agony on the cross, He cried out to His Father, "My God, My God, why have You forsaken Me?" (Matt. 27:46). And the heavens answered not a word. You would think the skies above would have been filled with thousands of angels descending upon Golgotha's hill and rescuing Jesus from His suffering. That's what I would have done, if it were my son. But God was silent. He was silent because behind the scenes He was fulfilling His purpose through the suffering of His Son to redeem us from sin. Once again His silence was His answer.

Why We Resent God

I must admit that for much of my life I've lost sight of what Mary and Martha were holding on to in their affliction: the assurance of God's love. Often when I've suffered loss I've felt abandoned, set aside, and forgotten. And yes, I have shaken my fist toward heaven and cried out in quiet desperation for relief. When the answers did not come the way I expected, first self-pity set in and then disappointment. I came to a place where I was living with an undercurrent of resentment toward God because I felt Him responsible for denying me the simplest ordinary happiness. For years the roadblock of resentment remained just under the surface of my faith, revealing itself whenever I experienced pain. This resentment took root because, unlike Mary and Martha, I lost sight of God's immeasurable love for me in my times of affliction. I always entered into seasons of sifting with an assurance of His love but when trouble lingered on indefinitely I questioned the validity of that same love. As I said in an earlier chapter, it's not the sting of loss that's so painful, it's the longevity of the thing.

That's the rub, isn't it? You sing the Shema when you've been pushed and shoved into a corner, and in the midst of the madness affirm His great love for you—"the one You love is sick." You hope and pray and praise and trust, and in your desperation even try to make deals with God. But the healing doesn't come, doors close rather than open, and one messenger after another brings bad news that gouges out another piece of your confidence and with it tiny morsels of your dignity. That marriage you believed could survive the Great San Francisco Earthquake? It's crumbling, because your spouse is asking, in disappointment, "Are you the one, or should I look for someone else?" Even the thought of the moral fiber of God—the standard-bearer of empathy—becomes a resentment, because He doesn't seem to be showing an ounce of concern for you. And somehow in the angst of it all you sense you're being transformed into the verminous creature in Franz Kafka's *The Metamorphosis* because you're losing a bit of yourself each day.

I'll tell you what I think: I think more and more people are living with resentment toward God that's just under the surface of their faith, revealing itself whenever they experience pain or even the annulment of ordinary happiness. They can't admit this because they think it would be blasphemous. So they keep on living their lives with pain covered by the shadows, trusting God on the outside—"All is well!"—but doubting His credibility on the inside. Consider this: if resilience seems far away to you, a fleeting hope, you might be fostering an underlying resentment toward God. I know this because I lived . . . no, not lived, but existed . . . for years resenting God.

For God's Sake, Where Is God?

Historians say there was not one Jew who survived the death camps with their faith unaltered. After experiencing such terrible human suffering it's no wonder Jewish people have ever since begged the question, "Where was God when our people were being slaughtered?" Elie Wiesel survived both the Auschwitz and Buchenwald concentration camps. His book *Night* is a record of the horrors of the camps, the memory of the loss of his family, and the theft of his childhood innocence. In it he recalls the day the Nazis hung three Jewish prisoners from the gallows. One of them was a young child.

> The head of the camp read the verdict. All eyes were on the child. He was pale, almost calm, but he was biting his lips as he stood in the shadow of the gallows . . . silent. "Where is merciful God, where is He?" someone behind me was asking. At the signal the three chairs were tipped over. Total silence in the camp. On the horizon, the sun was setting. "Caps off!" screamed the Lageralteste. His voice quivered. As for the rest of us, we were weeping. "Cover your heads!" Then came the march past the victims. The two men were no longer alive. . . . But the third rope was still moving: the child, too light, was still breathing. . . . And so he remained for more than half an hour, lingering between life and death, writhing before our eyes. And we were forced to look at him at close range. He was still alive when I passed him. His tongue was still red, his eyes not yet extinguished. Behind me, I heard the same man asking, "For God's sake, where is God?" And from within me, I heard a voice answer: "Where is He? This is where—hanging here from this gallows."[4]

The God Who Suffers with Us

Many have debated these words of Elie Wiesel. What did he mean? Some say Wiesel bought into the "death of God" theology embraced by many secular Jews after the Holocaust. But this goes against the fact that by his own admission Elie admits his faith was wounded but not destroyed in the death camps. How is it, then, that God was hanging from the gallows of a Jewish concentration camp? I think in this profound line Wiesel is actually unveiling a biblical truth that puts all suffering in perspective as it relates to God. By painting this picture of God on the gallows, Wiesel removes the possibility of any justification in resenting God because of suffering. This truth is found in the first part of Isaiah 63:9. There are just seven words in the line but they will profoundly change the way you think of God: "In all their affliction He was afflicted."

This means every time Israel suffered—and this includes four hundred years of slavery in Egypt, droughts, oppressive enemies, famines, captivities, and the like—God was there with them in the midst of all their afflictions. So, for God's sake, where is God? He is hanging from the gallows with afflicted people. He is the God who suffers. When you hurt He hurts. Where is God? This is where: hanging from the gallows with you.

We don't generally picture God in this way. We are more likely to perceive Him as distant, unacquainted with grief, and immune to our aching. But that's not how the Bible portrays Him.

> He is despised and rejected by men,
> A Man of sorrows and acquainted with grief.
> And we hid, as it were, our faces from Him;
> He was despised, and we did not esteem Him.
> Surely He has borne our griefs
> And carried our sorrows;
> Yet we esteemed Him stricken,
> Smitten by God, and afflicted.
> But He was wounded for our transgressions,
> He was bruised for our iniquities;
> The chastisement for our peace was upon Him,
> And by His stripes we are healed. (Isa. 53:3–5)

There is something about the character and capacity of God that requires Him to suffer with us. If God is love, and He is, then to view Him as unfeeling and uncaring would be to erase His very essence. If God doesn't suffer with us in our affliction, then God is not love, and if God is not love He ceases to exist. God does not love us in order to fulfill some selfish otherworldly need within His being. He loves us altruistically by giving us the gift of Himself—His goodness and lovingkindness—without expecting anything in return.

The most accurate and articulate picture of the nature of God is found in the crucifixion of Jesus. Theologian C. A. Dinsmore conveys the understanding of a God who suffers in these beautiful words:

> There was a cross in the heart of God before there was one planted on the green hill outside of Jerusalem. And now that the cross of wood has been taken down, the one in the heart of God abides, and it will remain so long as there is one sinful soul for whom to suffer.[5]

Hymn writer Charles Wesley put music to the idea of a suffering God: "Amazing love! How can it be that Thou, my God, shouldst die for me?"[6]

Where is God? This is where: hanging from this gallows.

The Fellowship of Suffering

The quaint town of Colmar is nestled in the countryside of Alsace, France. It is home to the Unterlinden Museum, which holds one of the world's greatest cultural treasures of art, the Isenheim Altarpiece. This painting depicts the crucifixion of Christ, brushed with such horror that some think it to be the most beautiful expression of ugliness in the world of art. Over five hundred years old, the painting was created by German artist Matthias Grunewald. Art historian Jonathan Jones describes Grunewald's masterpiece this way:

> The first thing you see, walking through the chilly gothic chapel towards Matthias Grunewald's Isenheim Altarpiece . . . is death. It is

death without disguise, grotesque and terrifying. The wooden cross to which the dead man is nailed has a three-dimensional, trompe l'oeil quality. Look at the wood: rough, cheap, ugly timbers have been crudely knocked together, as if the artist had asked a carpenter to make a mock-up. From this three-dimensional cross, the body of the dying man juts forward. His green fingers are twisted in horrible, grasping claws. This Christ is frightening, a dying man clutching at you, reaching desperately for help that never comes. Christ dies in a terrible, empty desert place, with low massifs in the distance, and a lightless light, a depressing, dreary, empty darkness. . . . Why did a medieval artist paint Christ in this shocking way?[7]

The answer to why Grunewald brushed such a repulsive portrait of Christ may well be found in the apostle Paul's pursuit to understand the depth of Christ's suffering for sin: "That I may know Him and the power of His resurrection, and the fellowship of His sufferings" (Phil. 3:10). Here is a surprising truth: we cannot have authentic fellowship with Christ apart from sharing in His sufferings.

Remember the two men on the road to Emmaus? Jesus was revealed to them in the breaking of the bread. They did not recognize Christ until He reached out and took a loaf of bread, broke it, and blessed it. What prompted the opening of their eyes? Was it the way He blessed the bread or the way He broke it? Or was it something more obvious? We know from the account of the crucifixion that Jesus was brutally beaten. The Romans shoved a crown of thorns on His brow so not only would Jesus's forehead have been pierced and scarred but His eyelids and face as well. Part of His beard was pulled out and He was repeatedly struck in the face. "Then some began to spit on Him, and to blindfold Him, and to beat Him, and to say to Him, 'Prophesy!' And the officers struck Him with the palms of their hands" (Mark 14:65). "Then they spat on Him, and took the reed and struck Him on the head" (Matt. 27:30). The "reed" used to batter Jesus's face was something like a wooden staff. Considering the fact that He was wearing the crown of thorns during the beating, that staff would have acted like a hammer, bludgeoning the thorns deeper into His skin, scarring and marring Him so severely and completely He would have been unrecognizable. That's why Isaiah says of Him, "there were many who were appalled at him—his appearance was so disfigured beyond that of any human being and his form marred beyond human likeness" (Isa. 52:14 NIV).

In the last chapter we talked about how the two men on the road to Emmaus were disappointed that Jesus was not the world-conquering hero they expected, which may have made it impossible for them to imagine Jesus with them. But it is also true that the scarring on Jesus's face was so ghastly the two could not recognize him. Maybe the same scars are what prevented Mary Magdalene from knowing who He was at the empty tomb; she thought He was the gardener.

So how did the two men sitting at the dinner table with Jesus finally come to identify Him? I think it was His hands. When Jesus reached out and took the bread and broke it, they saw the nail prints in His hands. He was revealed to them in His suffering. Maybe this is why Thomas didn't say to Jesus, "My Lord and my God!" (John 20:28) until after he saw and touched the wounds in his hands and side. Maybe he was blinded by the horror of His appearance. If Jesus still bears the marks of suffering in His hands, would He not bear them in His face as well? It's a scandalous thought, but when we see Jesus face-to-face we will be appalled by His appearance because I believe He is eternally marred.

When I think of what He went through for me, I can never be offended toward Him in times of loss because resentment is the opposite of gratitude. Instead, I accept that whatever I am going through is actually bringing me into deeper fellowship with the God who suffers. There is a blessing that comes with this perspective. Jesus said, "Blessed is he who is not offended because of Me"

(Luke 7:23). The fellowship of sharing in the sufferings of Christ that Paul talks about is not one-sided. As I grow closer to Jesus through appreciating His sufferings, He grows closer to me through appreciating mine. He knows the pain I'm feeling because He feels my pain. That's why the psalmist can write, "The LORD is close to the brokenhearted and saves those who are crushed in spirit" (Ps. 34:18 NIV). That's why we find Jesus weeping at the tomb of His friend Lazarus; He felt Mary and Martha's pain.

Theologian Dennis Ngien writes about this fellowship of suffering we share with God:

> If it were not the very God himself who became sin and suffered for us, what hope of life is left? What God cannot participate in, he cannot redeem. If God has not entered into our suffering and death, then there is no hope for redemption of our pain. . . . God's loving vulnerability thus provides us with a model for Christian living in this world. Being vulnerable necessarily involves risk, pain and loss.[8]

The cross is a statement of who God is. The cross is the great scandal of time and eternity. A God who suffers is scandalous. The cross declares who God really is: ultimate love and mercy. The roadblock of resentment strategically attempts to cloak your perception of God as He is, hanging on the gallows. Why? Because if God actually suffers with you in your affliction there is no room for resentment. The only thing that gives life to resentment of God is the notion of divine impassibility, the idea that God can't connect with your suffering because He's divine and therefore unable to experience pain. In this view, Christ suffered in His humanity but not in His divinity. But 2 Corinthians 5:19 says, "God was in Christ reconciling the world to Himself." That was God on the cross in all of His divinity and humanity. If you don't know a God who hung helpless on hewn timber, you don't know God and will go on existing with resentment toward Him just under the surface of your faith. Could it be that some cannot bring themselves to accept the dreadfulness and scandal of God on the cross because it forces them to realize their own dreadfulness without Him?

Where is God? This is where: hanging from this gallows.

Resentment Traps

The truth that Christ suffers when you suffer should remove any present or future resentment toward the One who "sympathize[s] with our weaknesses" (Heb. 4:15). When a person is resentful of God they become ensnared, trapped, and tripped up. Resentment works as a roadblock placed in your way to impede your progress.

A person who resents God has come to the point of distrusting the validity and credibility of the One he or she ought to follow. In short, it is a disapproval of the wisdom of God behind His decisions concerning your life and future. Ultimately, if you resent God you will be roadblocked from, at the very least, acknowledging His divine authority in your life, let alone responding in agreement with His will.

Resentment traps come in all shapes and sizes. The enemy of your soul is a clever hunter and baits the traps with tasty trifles of self-pity and feelings of disappointment. He seeks a platform to scandalize you (entrap you) by accusing Jesus's ministry toward you: "Just look at what a dedicated servant you have been to Christ, and what do you have to show for it? Now that the pressure is on, where is He? He led you down this dead-end street and then abandoned you. When are you going to wake up to the fact He's uninterested in meeting your needs? He's really treating you poorly. You're really going to have to go it alone—that's right!—self-sufficiency is your only hope of survival." Sound familiar?

Though you may not perceive it, you are actually surrounded by subtle resentment traps, carefully placed snares that seek to ambush any hope of recovery. In fact, you may already be ensnared and don't know it. Remember our four roadblocks: self-pity, disappointment, resentment, and indecisiveness? Self-pity leads to disappointment and disappointment to resentment, and the endgame is indecisiveness. You will know if you have tripped the trigger of a resentment trap whenever you have the slightest uncertainty—a kind of low-grade humming vacillation—about God's boundless love for you. When you tend to pause at the point of trusting, the sharp teeth of a resentment trap may have already pierced your soul and indecisiveness is setting up the final roadblock to your resilience.

God Will Sometimes Challenge Your Mind to Get to Your Heart

To keep you from living with resentment toward Him, God will sometimes challenge your mind in order to expose what's in your heart. God often asked extraordinary things of His chosen people or asked them to believe Him when the human mind might just rebel. Here's an example from John's Gospel:

> [Jesus said,] "I am the living bread which came down from heaven. If anyone eats of this bread, he will live forever; and the bread that I shall give is My flesh, which I shall give for the life of the world."
>
> The Jews therefore quarreled among themselves, saying, "How can this Man give us His flesh to eat?"
>
> Then Jesus said to them, "Most assuredly, I say to you, unless you eat the flesh of the Son of Man and drink His blood, you have no life in you." . . .
>
> Therefore many of His disciples, when they heard this, said, "This is a hard saying; who can understand it?" . . . From that time many of His disciples went back and walked with Him no more. (John 6:51–53, 60, 66)

These followers of Jesus were offended over something they didn't understand. When they left, Jesus asked His twelve disciples, "Do you also want to go away?" (v. 67). Simon Peter, who was probably just as confused about what Jesus was saying, answered, "Lord, to whom shall we go? You have the words of eternal life. Also we have come to believe and know that You are the Christ, the Son of the living God" (vv. 68–69).

For the first group of disciples, the challenge to their intellect revealed the unbelief in their hearts. For the second group, their response to Jesus's challenging statements revealed the faith in their hearts.

A season of loss can be perplexing because we thrive on being in the know and having all the answers. But we simply don't have all the information and we never will; nobody does. Often, a lack of understanding of what God is doing and why He's doing it can breed resentment. So God asks challenging things of us sometimes, giving us a glimpse of the alcoves of our hearts. That glimpse will tell us whether we're following Him in belief or unbelief. I love Peter's answer: "Lord, to whom shall we go? You have the words of eternal life" (v. 68). Peter called Jesus "Lord," which is the word *kurios* in Greek and signifies that the person being addressed is worthy to be followed.

Peter did not resent God because of Jesus's challenging statements. Instead, he confessed he didn't have any other option but to follow Him as Lord, trusting fully in His wisdom. Without having all the pieces of the puzzle, Peter believed anyway. And this is the place where God is leading you: to realize you have no other option but to follow. To the point where you press on regardless of what God is doing and why He's doing it, and through it all: times of loss and sorrow, bad reports and past-due mortgage bills, divorce papers served at your office where everybody sees your tears, and sudden phone calls with anxious, crying voices asking you if you're sitting down. Through all those things, your season of sifting actually becomes a joy because your fellowship with Him—that mutual suffering we talked about—has taken on an entirely new meaning. You've actually become content in the crucible. You are so conscious of His presence, and so confident in His love and your ultimate resilience through Him, you're not obsessing over your prolonged season of aching. In fact, you begin to experience the peculiar inclination—a secret wish, perhaps—to remain in a place of need because your fellowship with Christ has never been as satisfying. It's in this place of fellowship that old, reinforced roadblocks of resentment toward God are finally removed.

Because I became resentful of God in my childhood, I spent what has seemed like ten lifetimes holding on to other options in my relationship with Him. For most of my life I've been like the first group of disciples who just walked away. I successfully cloaked my resentment toward Him publicly while privately being compromised in my faith. But God in His mercy did not allow me to continue on in unbelief, doubting His love and questioning His wisdom. So He challenged my mind in order to reveal my heart, and in the end, my resentment toward Him and the roadblock to my resilience it fashioned dissolved.

I'll tell you my story in chapter 9, but first we're going to look at the final roadblock to resilience, indecisiveness. It's the final destination of where self-pity, disappointment, and resentment lead, and it has drowned many in its wake. It's a stronghold well described by Seneca the Younger: "Most men ebb and flow in wretchedness between the fear of death and the hardship of life; they are unwilling to live, and yet they do not know how to die."

When you get this overpowering roadblock of indecisiveness out of your way, you'll be ready to start planning your comeback!

Why We Can Take Our Next Breath

We opened this chapter with a discussion about how the Holocaust caused so many to be resentful of God and ask the question, "Where was God?" Jewish actor Géza Röhrig starred in a movie about the Holocaust, *Son of Saul*, and he has something to say to us about being resentful of God because of our suffering:

> But it wasn't God who rounded up the Jews and the Gypsies and the Soviet POWs and the gays and the perfectly German mental patients and the perfectly German midgets and slaughtered them. We did it. The human family did it. . . . He could and should have stopped it at a much earlier stage. But I would not be able to get up from my bed in the morning, let alone pray, if I didn't fully believe that God somehow was there holding the hands of each and every Jew in the gas chamber. I think there is room for me to believe, as irrational as it sounds, that since God is all-capable, in some mysterious way, He suffered along and was there. If I wasn't able to believe this, I don't know why I'd take my next breath.[9]

BOUNCE TAKEAWAY:
Reflect on Your Own Story

1. Have you ever experienced loss and as a result developed resentment toward God? As you look back, can you remember the circumstance that inspired the sense of resentment? If so, what happened?

2. In this chapter we discussed the vulnerability of God and His willingness to suffer with us when we experience pain and heartache. How has this view of the nature and character of God changed your perspective of your own journey through seasons of suffering?

3. As you think back over your life journey and remember the times you resented God, do you think it was because you didn't have all the information about what God was doing and why He was doing it? As you face future uncertainties

without having all the information, how can you keep yourself from falling into the trap of resenting God?

BOUNCE CHALLENGE #7

It's very important at this point of your journey that your heart experiences healing from all resentment toward God. If you have been ensnared by resentment, the Holy Spirit can gently open the trap and set you free. Perhaps, because of events out of your control, you may be enduring pain caused by the sharp teeth of such a trap piercing your soul. I encourage you to pen a prayer in your bounce journal at this time. Ask the Lord to help you let go of the resentment and heal you of the pain it has caused.

8

Indecisiveness

Sempronius and the Forty Singing Wrestlers

Until one is committed, there is hesitancy, the chance
to draw back, always ineffectiveness. Concerning all
acts of initiative (and creation), there is one elementary
truth, the ignorance of which kills countless ideas and
splendid plans: that the moment one definitely commits
oneself, then Providence moves too. All sorts of things
occur to help one that would never otherwise have oc-
curred. A whole stream of events issues from the decision, raising in one's favour all manner of unforeseen
incidents and meetings and material assistance, which
no man could have dreamt would have come his way.

W. H. Murray, *The Scottish Himalaya Expedition*

Sometimes the decisions we make—or don't make—change
the course of history. Such is the story of the forty singing
wrestlers. Their lives and their bold decision have inspired most,

puzzled some, and troubled others for nearly two thousand years. What makes the story of their lives so riveting is that they decisively chose a slow and painful death rather than denounce Christianity. They pressed on regardless of death. Their decision was clear to them: Would they follow Christ, or would they live a life of self-loathing and emptiness brought on by their indecisiveness?

It was a war that started the wrestlers' story. Along the winding Danube River between the years 166 and 180 AD, the armies of Rome fought off an invasion. One battle in the long conflict stands out. Emperor Marcus Aurelius, the last of the good emperors, led the men of the Twelfth Legion against the men of Quadi. Cornered in a dry valley, the Romans fought valiantly but were outnumbered and outmaneuvered.

Tasting victory, the Quadians pulled back from the wounded Roman legion and waited for the blazing sun to finish what they had started. Cut off from water, the Roman soldiers grew weaker with each passing day. They prayed to their gods for rain.

As the sun grew more intense, it was reported to the emperor that within the legion was a small contingent of Christian soldiers, and if they were allowed to publicly pray to their Christ, perhaps He would send rain. The order was given to the Christians to call upon their God, and as they prayed, the heavens thundered and the clouds burst with life-giving water. With renewed strength, the Romans regained the initiative, broke through the Quadian blockade, and won the battle and eventually the war.

Because of that miracle, Emperor Aurelius gave an official name to this legion: *Legio XII Fulminata*, which means, "Twelfth Legion Armed with Lightning." He honored the Christian soldiers by issuing a decree forbidding the persecution of Christians throughout the Roman Empire. The Twelfth Legion Armed with Lightning represented the miracle of the rainstorm with a lightning bolt forged on the breast of their armor. Today, in the Piazza Colonna in Rome, Italy, stands the Column of Marcus Aurelius that commemorates the miracle of the lightning and rainstorm in the battle against Quadi.

Now, fast-forward to the freezing winter in the year 320. The Twelfth Legion Armed with Lightning was guarding an outpost in the city of Sebaste. The legion still retained a contingent of Christian soldiers nearly 150 years later. The pagan emperor, Licinius, despised Christians. Fearing his armies were being infiltrated by men of faithful devotion to Christ rather than to Rome, he sent out a decree to his military commanders demanding all soldiers offer sacrifices to the Roman gods and renounce their allegiance to Jesus—or die.

The edict made its way east and finally reached the Twelfth Legion Armed with Lightning in Sebaste. The governor of the region, Agricola, gathered the legionnaires together—a number somewhere between three and six thousand men—and read the decree from Emperor Licinius.

Within the ranks of the Twelfth Legion was a band of soldiers known as the Emperor's Wrestlers. They fought in the amphitheater of Rome and pledged their loyalty to the emperor, to protect him from danger and all threats to his authority. Before each contest they stood before the emperor's throne, and the forty wrestlers would sing, "We, the wrestlers, wrestling for thee, O Emperor, to win for thee the victory and from thee the victor's crown!" Over time, these forty wrestlers bent their knees to Jesus Christ. They could relate to the decisiveness and courage it took for Him to lay down His life for them.

When the decree was read by Agricola, the forty wrestlers stepped forward, and one from their number responded, "We have made a decision to follow Christ and serve Him only, and cannot sacrifice to other gods." The commander of the Twelfth Legion, Lysias, was ordered to strip the men of their armor, flog them, and cast them into a dungeon. But the forty wrestlers remained resolute in their decision.

A verdict then came down from Governor Agricola, and they were ordered to be led out at sundown, naked, to a frozen lake, where they would suffer a slow and terrible death. Lysias, having mercy for his soldiers, ordered that a bathhouse on the shore be prepared with warm water and stocked with bread just in case the men changed their minds. Fires were built next to the bathhouse in order to roast skewered meat. Lysias thought the warm bath, warm bread, and roasting meat would tempt the men to alter their decision and sacrifice to the gods of Rome.

A centurion named Sempronius stood at attention with a small company of men near the fires and the bathhouse. Should the wrestlers come to their senses and waver in their decision to follow Christ alone, they could warm themselves in the bathhouse, enjoy a delicious meal, and receive a full military pardon for their defiance of the emperor's decree. The only string attached, of course, was that they must sacrifice to the emperor's gods.

As the sun set over the hills of Sebaste, a song could be heard coming from the frozen lake: "Forty wrestlers, wrestling for Thee, O Christ, to win for Thee the victory and from Thee the victor's crown." At first, the volume of the voices was loud enough to pierce through the freezing air like lightning. But as the hours passed and the temperature plummeted, the voices became faint, like the sound of a distant train whistle gradually disappearing into the night. Sempronius and his men watched from the shore for any sign their comrades would relent. The scene from the wrestlers' viewpoint must have been alluring. The steam rising from the warm water of the bathhouse, the sight and smell of meat cooking on hot flames, and the silhouettes of Sempronius and his men standing guard in the firelight. And yet, no sound of surrender was heard, only a song now raised in a whisper: "Forty wrestlers, wrestling for Thee, O Christ, to win for Thee the victory and from Thee the victor's crown."

Did they waver in their decision? Did they run to the security and sanctuary of the bathhouse to save themselves? Did they perish on the frozen lake? And what became of Centurion Sempronius? The end of this story could either be one of the best accounts of decisiveness ever told or a disappointing, anticlimactic narrative about doublemindedness—but first I want to explain how indecisiveness, our final roadblock, frustrates your resilience.

If You're Indecisive You've Got Issues

One of the clearest definitions of indecisiveness in the Bible is found in James 1:5–8:

> If any of you lacks wisdom, let him ask of God, who gives to all liberally and without reproach, and it will be given to him. But let him ask in faith, with no doubting, for he who doubts is like a wave of the sea driven and tossed by the wind. For let not that man suppose that he will receive anything from the Lord; he is a double-minded man, unstable in all his ways.

The word *doubleminded*, as it is applied in the Bible, comes from the Greek word *dipsuchos*. We discover the meaning of *dipsuchos* when we break it down: from *di* we get "twice" and from *psuche* we get "a soul." To be doubleminded, then, simply means to have two minds or two souls that are in conflict with each other. It's clear that indecisiveness is a matter of your soul: your mind, will, and emotions. In short, it's a heart issue. If part of you trusts that God's love is perfect and His wisdom is infallible even in your suffering, and the other part of you has lost all hope in God's ability to restore your losses, you've got a vacillating heart. You've become "two-souled," or doubleminded. James makes it clear that indecisiveness is a matter of the heart when he says, "Draw near to God and He will draw near to you. Cleanse your hands, you sinners; and purify your hearts, you double-minded" (4:8).

You see, indecisiveness is much deeper than an elementary weakness in your decision-making capabilities. Indecisiveness cannot be solved by reading a how-to book about becoming more resolute. James says that indecisiveness is caused by an impurity in your heart. In other words, indecisiveness is sin: "Cleanse your hands, you sinners; and purify your hearts, you double-minded."

The Bible breaks sin down into three categories: sin, transgression, and iniquity. The psalmist David said, "I acknowledged my sin to You, and my iniquity I have not hidden. I said, 'I will confess my transgressions to the LORD,' and You forgave the iniquity of my sin" (Ps. 32:5).

First of all, David says, "I acknowledged my sin." Anything that separates you from the glory of God is sin. Basically, sin is like an archer who misses his mark: it's falling short of God's standard of righteousness. Next, David says, "I will confess my transgressions to the LORD." A transgression is a premeditated, repeated sin driven by willful disobedience. So when you miss the mark of God's righteousness, you have sinned. When you continue in that same sin over and over again, the sin becomes a transgression.

Continuing to lay out the categories of sin, David concludes by saying, "And You forgave the iniquity of my sin." An iniquity takes root in your life when sin gives birth to continued transgression. When that transgression is repeated long enough, it perverts and defiles your character—that's iniquity. Iniquity affects your beliefs and attitudes to the point where you become so entrenched in unbelief that hope evaporates. Iniquity destabilizes your inner equilibrium, and as a result you literally lose your willingness to choose. I believe iniquity is behind doublemindedness, because James tells us that a doubleminded man is "unstable in all his ways" (James 1:8).

Feed the Right Beast

You may be wondering why I chose four roadblocks to resilience. Why not five or ten? And why these specific four? The reason is

I have lived them. Through a series of events that I'll tell you about in the next chapter, I first allowed self-pity a place at the dinner table of my soul. We dined together as I lay my head on my pillow each night, thinking about my situation and receiving solace from my newfound friend. Before long, self-pity invited disappointment, and now there were two. "Certainly, you've got room for more guests," they said. And then the unthinkable happened. Without an invitation from me, they brought resentment toward God and my heart became corrupted with a deeply embedded distrust of God's love for me. Before long I was filled with bitter unbelief in God's ability to help me come back and recover from my loss.

Now there were three hungry guests at my table. Gradually, my resentment turned to outright rage toward God—subtly, of course—just under the surface where no one except my three new friends could see. But what I didn't completely recognize all along was that lurking in the shadows of the dining room in my heart was another figure. I would see glimpses of him from time to time but paid little attention. The more I nourished self-pity, disappointment, and resentment, the clearer the figure became. With each passing month he would slither a little farther from the shadows. His name was indecisiveness, and by the time I understood who he really was it was too late.

What I failed to comprehend was that by continually feeding my first three guests I was actually giving in to the sin of unbelief. Yes, the Bible makes it clear that unbelief is sin: "See to it, brothers and sisters, that none of you has a sinful, unbelieving heart that turns away from the living God" (Heb. 3:12 NIV). Because of my ongoing, willful choice to disbelieve in God's sovereign purpose in my life, my sin of unbelief became a transgression and ultimately an iniquity. My heart was now distorted and I became destabilized in my thinking and perceptions. I slowly came to the place where I ceased being a participant in my own destiny.

And then it happened. I looked up and there he was. Indecisiveness was seated at the head of my table with a sinister smile on his face, enjoying the feast I had prepared. Now there were four. The roadblocks fully in place, I entered into a dark season of complete doublemindedness, unable to make a decision to bounce back.

There's a tale about an old Cherokee man who was teaching his grandchildren about the deep issues of life. He said, "Every day there are two ravenous beasts—wolflike creatures—that tear and claw at each other within my heart. One of the beasts represents self-pity, envy, anger, guilt, sorrow, and regret. The other beast represents hope, joy, resilience, faith, compassion, and trust." The old man looked at his grandchildren with a knowing gleam in his eye, and said, "The same two beasts are fighting within your hearts and within the hearts of every person everywhere." The children thought about their grandfather's story for a long time, and then one asked him, "Grandfather, which beast will win?" The wise man answered, "The one you feed."

The Lord of the Flies

They say the sound of the flies was deafening. In the aftermath of Civil War conflicts, as thousands of dead and wounded soldiers lay on the battlefields of places like Gettysburg and Bull Run, swarms of flies came searching for open wounds in which to lay their eggs. One of the ways the Bible describes our adversary, the devil, is with the name *Beelzebub*, which means, "Lord of the Flies."

Here's what often happens. You're cruising through a wonderful life. The sun is shining, birds are singing, and even the stoplights turn green when you get close to the intersections. But suddenly your high expectations are met with disaster. An unexpected event rearranges your world, and unconsciously, without perceiving it, your initial commitment to resilience—that old faithful endurance under pressure—gives way to self-pity, disappointment, and resentment toward God. These roadblocks to your bounce-back are like open wounds the Lord of the Flies uses to sow seeds of doubt into your soul. The ultimate aim of the enemy is to bring you to a place of doubleminded indecisiveness where you are so overwhelmed with the shame of your loss you haven't the resolve to bounce back. This is why I believe the ultimate root of indecisiveness is shame.

When the Lord of the Flies plants shame within our souls it affects every area of our lives, especially our resolve. Let me show you how shame blockades our ability to make difficult but necessary decisions. When the enemy is successful in bringing you to a place of shame over a loss, he now begins to sow fear into that open wound of shame. Not only are you dealing with self-hate because of shame but now you are experiencing fear in decision making because if you fail you fear your self-hate will grow even worse. So you stay in a neutral and isolated place, avoiding shame and rejection by avoiding decisions that might cause others to question your character, motivation, or wisdom. Shame acts like a chalkboard eraser, wiping away fragments of your true self every day.

Elvis Has Left the Building

Now, let's look once again at our passage from James 1:5–8 to find out why indecisiveness is so destructive. First of all, James says that if you are two-souled or doubleminded, you are "like a wave of the sea driven and tossed by the wind" (v. 6). You suffer from the loss of identity, personal freedom, and dignity and are unable to decide for yourself; you have abdicated yourself. *Abdication* is best defined as stepping down, quitting, yielding responsibility, abandoning your post, and surrendering. If the roadblock of indecisiveness has brought you to the point of surrendering your divine appointment and purpose in life, then Elvis has left the building—and you're Elvis.

Next, James tells us, "For let not that man suppose that he will receive anything from the Lord" (v. 7). Now you're dealing with the loss of supernatural provision and insight. Sadly, you have come to the place where you are living in the gray area of assumption. This is a place that not only lacks wisdom but discernment as well. Think of it: James says if you are indecisive, you can't receive anything from the Lord. How can you ever hope to break free from self-pity, disappointment, resentment toward God, and indecisiveness if you cannot receive a desperately needed supply of God's supernatural wisdom and provision for your journey out of bondage?

Finally, James concludes that if you are doubleminded, you are "unstable in all [your] ways" (v. 8). You are facing the loss of moral clarity and a sense of divine purpose. At this point, you have lost all forward movement because you have ceased to be a participant in your own destiny.

Healing the Bruise

If you have been stripped of your identity, personal freedom, dignity, supernatural provision, discernment, moral clarity, and sense of divine purpose, you are dealing with an iniquity. What's iniquity, again? Iniquity is a kind of sin that defiles and weakens your character to the point where you have lost the wisdom it takes to make moral choices. Iniquity is a deep inner bruise that just won't heal or a festering wound that won't close. If these things describe your life circumstance, there is hope. In speaking of Jesus, Isaiah says, "He was wounded for our transgressions, He was bruised for our iniquities" (Isa. 53:5). This means Jesus was wounded for your wounds and bruised for your bruises. As well, if shame is holding you back from a decisive comeback because of the fear of failure, please know that Jesus defeated shame so it wouldn't defeat you. "Jesus, the author and finisher of our faith . . . for the joy that was set before Him endured the cross, despising the shame, and has sat down at the right hand of the throne of God" (Heb. 12:2).

The Lord desires to heal your inner bruises and close your open, festering wounds in order to prevent the Lord of the Flies from accomplishing his diabolical purpose, sowing unbelief and shame into your soul and causing doubleminded indecisiveness.

Now, for the Rest of the Story

The forty soldiers of Sebaste had been stripped naked and led by guards to the middle of a frozen lake to either die of the cold or recant and be ushered to the safety of the bathhouse by the centurion Sempronius and his men. As night temperatures fell, the forty soldiers could be heard faintly singing, "Forty wrestlers, wrestling for Thee, O Christ, to win for Thee the victory and from Thee the victor's crown." Toward the middle of the night Sempronius heard a voice that grew closer. Suddenly, out of the darkness he could see a man crawling on the ice. Sempronius ran to the half-frozen man, picked him up, and carried him to the bathhouse. The warm water was unable to save him, and in a few moments he perished.

Sempronius sank in despair. He ran back to his post, his eyes squinting, searching the blackness, thinking others might follow the frozen man to the shore. *Perhaps the next one will survive*, he thought, but all he heard was the hushed song of the wrestlers, this time with a lyric change: "Thirty-nine wrestlers, wrestling for Thee, O Christ, to win for Thee the victory and from Thee the victor's crown." Tears rolled down the face of Centurion Sempronius, and as they did he stepped away from the fire to conceal his grief from the other soldiers nearby. He had fought side by side with the wrestlers in fierce battles. They were brothers drawn together by war, with sword, spear, shield, and armor that all bore the same engraved lightning bolt from heaven.

What Lysias, the commander of the Twelfth Legion Armed with Lightning, didn't know was that one of his commanders—Sempronius himself—was more than a brother-in-arms to the thirty-nine soldiers still dying on the frozen lake. He was a brother in Christ. When Governor Agricola read the decree that all legionnaires must sacrifice to Roman gods or die, Sempronius was overwhelmed with indecisiveness. He felt empty when the forty wrestlers stepped forward and declared their faith, deciding he would rather live in the middle than die on the edge. Perhaps he had grown weary in his faith. Perhaps he had allowed an iniquity to weaken his resolve. Perhaps, through a series of events, he was feeding the beasts of self-pity, disappointment, and resentment toward God. Perhaps he had placed indecisiveness at the head of the table of his heart and had become doubleminded. But as the watches of the night passed and he listened to the songs of his fellow believers, he realized the thirty-nine remaining wrestlers had more faith in their dying than he had in his living. In other words, they knew how to die better than he knew how to live.

Faced with the prospect of living a compromised existence somewhere in the middle of an indecisive nowhere, Sempronius came to the boldest decision of his life. He shouted into the cold and bitter darkness, "I follow Jesus Christ! I am a Christian." It might have been the first time in his life he said something he really meant, and it felt good. With joy on his face and floods of tears running down his cheeks, he stripped off his armor and his clothes and ran toward the edge of the frozen lake to join the thirty-nine singing wrestlers. The men he left behind on the shore stood by his discarded armor, its forged emblem of a lightning bolt reflecting in the firelight, in wonder and astonishment. Suddenly, the song of the wrestlers was heard once again, and the voice of Sempronius, the elite centurion of the Twelfth Legion Armed with Lightning, was heard above the others: "Forty wrestlers, wrestling for Thee, O Christ, to win for Thee the victory and from Thee the victor's crown."

Sempronius died that night with the thirty-nine singing wrestlers. The next day the frozen bodies of the forty soldiers were burned, and their bones cast into a nearby river.

You would think that would be the end of the story. But in fact it's just the beginning. That night the Christians of Sebaste, under the cover of darkness, recovered the remains of the thirty-nine wrestlers and their fellow believer Sempronius on the shore of a bend where the river turned. They sent the bones to several cities throughout the Roman Empire, along with the record of what had happened to the forty decisive soldiers in Sebaste. The believers were memorializing the decisiveness, without vacillation, of these men in their choice to follow Christ.

What happened next is amazing. The story of the forty soldiers became a lightning rod of inspiration for believers facing constant persecution. Eventually, churches were built in honor of the forty men who stood against indecisiveness and chose to follow Christ even unto death. Among the churches dedicated to the memory of these men are the Holy Forty Martyrs Church in Veliko Tarnovo, Bulgaria; the Church of Forty Martyrs of Sebaste, Macedonia; the Armenian Cathedral in Aleppo, Syria; the Churches of St. Sophia in Ohrid, Macedonia, and Kiev, Ukraine; and the Chapel of the Forty Martyrs in the Church of the Holy Sepulcher in Jerusalem, Israel.

They Never Build Statues for Critics

I first heard about the forty martyrs of Sebaste as a teenager through the song "Forty Brave Soldiers for Jesus," written by Tom and Candy Green. To this day, that song and the tale behind it inspire me to remain resolute in my faith. Recently the legend of these martyrs was portrayed in a film called *The 40*. The film inspires Christians to be decisive when faced with persecution and difficult choices. The fact that this story is still alive tells me one thing for sure: decisive people are long remembered and indecisive people soon forgotten.

I once was struggling with a tough decision that was bound to make some people unhappy. A wise friend counseled me to do what I believed was the right thing, no matter the cost, because, he said, "They never build statues for critics." And that's true. History remembers people who do the right thing regardless of what others think. History remembers the thirty-nine wrestlers and Centurion Sempronius but can't seem to recall the indecisive soldier who crawled back to the safety of the shore—which wasn't safe at all. One of the first things I want to do when I get to heaven is to meet the brave singing wrestlers of the Twelfth Roman Legion Armed with Lightning and tell them their unfaltering decisiveness was not in vain because it inspired me and countless others to believe that a life lived in doublemindedness is no life at all.

Security Is Overrated

When it really comes down to it, security is overrated. Think about it: What is the greater risk? Staying where you are in an indecisive, protective bubble, stuck in the center of a suffocating, miserable parentheses, or venturing out to an uncertain steep cliff edge overlooking new possibilities?

The answer? You're not as secure and safe as you think you are. In fact, you're not safe at all. Why? Because it's a greater risk to live in a state of hesitant mediocrity than to breathe freedom's fresh air on the other side of the barriers of self-pity, disappointment, resentment toward God, and indecisiveness. When those roadblocks are in your rearview mirror, you'll live. If you spend the rest of your life staring at them from your front windshield, you'll eventually be smothered to death. In the words of William Wallace from the motion picture *Braveheart*:

Every man dies; not every man truly lives. . . . Sons of Scotland, I am William Wallace . . . and I see a whole army of my countrymen here in defiance of tyranny. You've come to fight as free men and free men you are. What will you do without freedom? . . . Fight and you may die. Run and you'll live, at least awhile. And dying in your beds many years from now, would you be willing to trade all the days from this day to that for one chance, just one chance, to come back here and tell our enemies that they can take our lives but they'll never take our freedom?[1]

Lessons from a Biscuit

Now that we have identified the four obstructions to your comeback, it's time to discover your resilience plan. Here's a wonderful lead-in to the final part of our journey toward resilience from one of my favorite books, *Seabiscuit: An American Legend*, by Laura Hillenbrand. It's the story of a little racehorse that, against all odds, became a legend. Here are a few of my favorite lines from the book:

Like Smith, Woolf, and Pollard, he believed that the match was not going to be determined by speed. The deciding factor would be resolve. One of the horses was going to crack in the homestretch. The other would come home the undisputed champion of American racing.[2]

The broken-legged jockey began the period of his life that he would call "a long hard pull." Red would go up to the barn, hitch a lead rope onto Seabiscuit, and head off into the meadows, swinging painfully along on his crutches while Seabiscuit limped beside him. "We were a couple of old cripples together," Red said, "all washed up. But somehow we both had a pretty good idea that we'd be back."[3]

All Smith had to cling to was a wild thought that Seabiscuit might someday return. . . . A reporter walked up. "Wouldn't it be great,"

119

the newsman said, "if the Biscuit could stage a comeback?" Smith slid up in his chair. "I suppose," he said, an edge to his voice, "you think he won't come back?" The reporter, flustered, stammered out something about the rarity of successful comebacks. Smith stood up. "The Biscuit will come back," he said in a voice more emotional than he meant it to be. "He'll come back and fool the whole turf world."[4]

You're going to bounce back too!

BOUNCE TAKEAWAY:
Reflect on Your Own Story

1. Think back over your life and explore whether or not the four roadblocks to resilience (self-pity, disappointment, resentment toward God, and indecisiveness) have ever gained a place at the table of your heart. If so, how have they hindered your destiny?

2. I said in this chapter that the ultimate root of indecisiveness is shame. Can you identify any shame or self-hate within your heart? Was it due to harmful words someone spoke over you? Perhaps a failure that became an open wound in which the "Lord of the Flies" sowed seeds of shame and guilt? Could it have been a hidden sin, or something else? Take some time to think about this.

3. Can you recall a time in your life story when indecisiveness was a roadblock? What happened that caused you to start moving again?

BOUNCE CHALLENGE #8

Take a risk! If you're hesitant to move forward because you've been blocked by indecisive doublemindedness, then it's time to break free. In your bounce journal list the four resilience blockers:

1. Self-Pity
2. Disappointment
3. Resentment toward God
4. Indecisiveness

After each roadblock I would like you to write: "Free in Jesus's name!" Now write these four words: "I have decided to . . ." Now list five things you have taken to heart in our exploration together so far. For example, you could say something like:

I HAVE DECIDED TO:

1. Press on regardless of my circumstance (describe the circumstance).
2. Ask the Lord to deliver me from shame.
3. Take a risk and step out in faith and try a new thing I feel impressed the Lord wants me to do. This new thing is: (describe your new adventure).

PART 3

Your
Resilience
Plan

9

Liquidate Some Mental Real Estate

Yet Why Not Say What Happened?

> A memoir should have some uplifting quality, inspiring
> or illuminating, and that's what separates a life story
> that can influence other people.
>
> Mitch Albom, "Mitch Albom Explains
> the Art of Storytelling"

Pat Conroy, author of *The Prince of Tides* and *The Great Santini*, once said: "One of the greatest gifts you can get as a writer is to be born into an unhappy family. I could not have been born into a better one."[1] We are all in some way glimpses of our childhood experiences. The great pity of growing up is we tend to categorize our memories. The pleasurable ones we save and tuck away for periodic instant recall. The ones that bring us pain we try to effectively erase, like cleaning a computer hard drive.

I worry about people who have forgotten their past. The things that happened to you in your life story—the good, the bad, the beautiful, and the ugly—are all parts of who you are, for better or for worse. If I have buried the truth of my story, I become but a shell of a person living in denial of the human experience with all of its pain and pleasure. For many, painful memories are like unseen tent pegs driven deep into their souls, tethering the bonds of their reluctant encampments. They long to move on as sojourners, but because of an unwillingness to understand their stories, they eventually become settlers, surrounded by so much mental baggage they can't go anywhere.

The fact is you simply cannot hope a painful story away. You cannot work it away, either. I see people attempting both. They choose to live in denial of their pain, or through some kind of penitence try to make it disappear through work. However, neither denial nor penitence help heal a wounded soul.

What's the answer? Should I spend the rest of my days rehearsing my painful past? No, of course not. Yet I cannot pull up the tent pegs of my pain until I find the meaning for what I've endured. A wonderful truth of the Lord's healing is that it usually comes when I acknowledge I'm suffering from past issues. I think that's why Jesus asked wounded people where it hurt.

It's Time to Tell Your Story

If you've become a settler in suffering, it's time to become a sojourner, pull up the tent pegs, and move on. Liquidating some mental real estate is the first step in your resilience plan. You need to find the meaning for what has happened to you, and in finding that meaning you'll find healing. A good place to start is to write your story. This statement, which has been attributed to several authors, rings true to me: "We don't write to be understood; we write to understand."

There is plenty of research that proves writing your story is one of the best ways to kick-start your resilience. Placing a blank piece of paper in front of yourself and writing down your story—the good, the bad, and the ugly—can be daunting, maybe even downright nerve-racking. Think of the psalms of David. These are gut-wrenching journals of his pains, fears, and longings. When I think of a character in the Bible who had extraordinary self-understanding, emotional intelligence, and an incredible capacity for resilience, I think of David. Somewhere in writing those inspired journals, David found the reason for his suffering and, eventually, resilience.

Forgiveness Is Like the Scent the Rose Sheds on the Heel That Crushes It

I once wrote a book entitled *The Forgotten Blessing*. It's about overcoming transgenerational verbal abuse. Though I did not disclose it at the time because my abuser was still living, I wrote the book out of my own pain from a childhood in which I was continually verbally assaulted. God used the experience of writing to help me understand my own story and the purpose behind it. I came to realize, when the book was finished, that by helping others find healing from the abuse of a cursing tongue I also found my own healing. They say that forgiveness is like the scent the rose sheds on the heel that crushes it—and that was true for me. It was easier for me to forgive and begin living my life without regrets when I accepted that what had happened to me was something God could use to bless others. It was understanding my story that gave me the nerve to bounce back.

Joseph is another Bible character who portrayed remarkable resilience. Sold into slavery by his jealous brothers, he would spend nearly twenty years in prison. He could have carried the mental baggage of bitterness with him the rest of his life, but he found meaning in his story when he blessed the very brothers who had cursed him. Promoted to second in command in the nation of

Egypt, Joseph was able to save the region from starvation. The same brothers who rejected him were saved too. At the end of Joseph's story, he told his brothers, "You intended to harm me, but God intended it for good to accomplish what is now being done, the saving of many lives" (Gen. 50:20 NIV).

Somehow, Joseph was able to liquidate the mental real estate of resentment that could have easily gained ground in his thinking, and in the process he found meaning for his suffering. Tell me: How would we have ever discovered the resilience of people like David and Joseph if we never heard their stories?

Yet Why Not Say What Happened?

My wife's sister, Carol, and Carol's husband, Ross, farm nearly ten thousand acres about an hour west of Chicago. They were the stereotypical all-American family until they suffered unspeakable pain. Their fifteen-year-old son, after learning his girlfriend was breaking up with him, took his own life down by their boathouse at the edge of the lake on their farm. For some years they were adrift. Carol's suffering was so deep she simply could not find her cadence. I suggested she write about the day her son committed suicide. She wrote around the day, but could not bring herself to pen the words about the moment she was awakened, in the early morning hours, by the sound of the gunshot, nor the experience of a mother finding her beautiful young son lying in the sand with a shotgun blast to his head.

Time passed. Then, one afternoon, she called me with the news that she had done it. She had faced her fear and recorded every detail. Somehow, in the journey she found meaning and healing and moved past the tragedy. Rather than digging in and settling down in an encampment filled with "why" and "if only" and shame-filled thoughts like *What will people think of us as parents?* she pulled up the tent pegs and moved to higher ground. She simply refused to allow the mental real estate of shame and regret to encroach upon her desire to bounce back from the dread.

Writing the painful details of her story marked the start of her comeback. She is now encouraging other moms who are facing the heart-wrenching pain of teenage suicide, speaking on Christian radio stations and at women's conferences, and writing a book about her family's tragedy. Yes, writing can help us understand our own lives, and it is why I'm asking you to write in your bounce journal.

One of my favorite poems is called "Epilogue," by Robert Lowell. It's about his inadequacy to describe in words what he actually feels. My favorite line from the poem is, "Yet why not say what happened?" And in that line is my challenge to you: "Yet why not say what happened?" Why not sit down at your computer, or with pen and paper, and write down your story in all of its ugliness and cruelty, and then, somehow, find the meaning of it all—the silver lining inside.

Some people wonder why God inspired biblical writers to tell stories about heartbreaking family conflicts. Think about it: after the flood Noah plants a vineyard, and after drinking a little too much wine he ends up drunk in his tent, and his son Ham uncovers his nakedness. The story of Jacob's rejection by his father, Isaac, is woven right into the middle of the family's story. David's adultery and his estrangement with his son Absalom reads like a soap opera. Why did God allow these stories and many others like them to be told? I think it is to help us make our way through the same kinds of tough issues and, in the end, just like the characters of the Bible, bounce back.

In this chapter, I'm going to tell you my story. It's not pretty, but if I tried to erase just one paragraph I would not be the person I am today. And here's a twist: If I never had anything to bounce back from, how could I, with confidence, encourage you to mount a comeback? I'm sure my story is less tragic than most and perhaps more tragic than others. The truth is, we're not on a grading scale here because our stories, no matter how painful or pleasurable—whether they read like a tragedy or a comedy—are ours, and to us they're real.

You don't tell your story to dredge up old hurts. Who needs that, right? You tell your story to figure out where you've come from so that you can realize—maybe for the first time—why you are on this planet. You tell your story to find that every moment from your past has meaning and purpose. Your story helps you experience the wonderful revelation that your life events are not just disconnected dots on a canvas but actually form a beautiful landscape that has both a shining noonday sun and the dark clouds of night's horizon. Bitterly cold and bleak winters, glorious springs, dry summers, and the fiery red and orange hues of fall are all wonderfully brushed into the same scene. You would think that meshing your joys and sorrows together in one artwork would be more surreal and abstract than realistic, but in reality the landscape of your life only makes sense when it's viewed in whole, not in part. The scene would only be confusing if you left out a piece of the puzzle.

When you write your story you'll find there is a continuity and rhythm to the events of your life. You tell your story because it helps you identify the mental scar tissue that has formed around the wounds from your past. Removing these hardened barnacles will be necessary before resilience can become a reality. At the end of the day, telling your story helps you liquidate some negative mental real estate you don't need to own anymore. So, here goes: my story, as raw and as vulnerable as I can tell it. Maybe telling my story will inspire you to tell yours.

My Story

There are only two things I remember about the man who brought me into this world: my father, William David Früh. The first memory is pleasurable. Sitting in a rocking chair before a redbrick fireplace surrounded by a white mantel, with the small fortress enclosing a roaring fire, my father held me in his arms and rocked me to sleep. I can still smell the freshly lain oak floors beneath his feet and hear the crackling of the dry eucalyptus logs, the slow ticking of the mantel clock, and the creaking sound the chair made against the planks, wood against wood. It's mysterious why you remember certain things. Why the smell of the floors, the sight of the red brick and white mantel, the creaking of the rocking chair, the popping of the fire, and the ticking of the clock? I'm not really sure, but maybe they represented to me the safety and security every child needs and the things most fathers want to provide.

The second memory I have of my father is from the night of December 23, 1961, when I was three years old. I remember sliding across the oak floors in my one-piece pajamas into my father's waiting arms. He looked at me with his deep, tender eyes and asked if I wanted to go on a ride over to church, where he and the other volunteers were packaging Christmas candy for the Christmas Eve service. And he was excited. Two days before, in the mail, my father had received something he had been expecting for a long time—his general contracting carpenter's license—and he wanted to tell his friends at church about it. My dad was a builder, and the oak floors, white mantel, and redbrick fireplace were his finishing touches to our new home. My father had spent years constructing homes for a large building firm in Carmel, California. Now he was venturing out on his own. My grandfather, a master carpenter in his own right, had taught my father well.

When you're a thirty-one-year-old carpenter at the beginning of the California building boom of the sixties, you've got the world on a string. Call it youthful exuberance or just plain risk taking, my father cashed in his life insurance policy, bought a piece of land, and began construction on five new homes. Ours was the first to be finished, just in time for Christmas. That's why I could still smell the varnish on the oak floors.

It was Saturday, early evening, when my dad carried me out the door in my pajamas to make the drive to the church, about ten minutes away. It was a Saturday etched into my memory. There was a cold chill in the air that December 23, and I don't know if it was the temperature that changed his mind or the thought that we wouldn't get back until after my bedtime, but my father brought me back into the house and told me I'd better stay home with my mother and my sister, Kathy, age five. I remember crying out to him as he walked out that door to his little Mercury Comet in the driveway, "Take me with you, Daddy!"

And then he turned and said the last words I would ever hear coming from his lips: "I'll be right back, son." But he never came back. He walked through that new door, down that new sidewalk, and onto that new driveway overlooking four other new houses that would soon have redbrick fireplaces and white mantels and maybe a ticking clock and a rocking chair or two, and perhaps another little boy sliding across freshly varnished oak floors, and he never returned.

Soon after my father pulled out of our subdivision onto Green Valley Road, a drunk driver traveling at high speed that Saturday night before Christmas Eve, 1961, took my father's life. They said the collision was so powerful he was killed instantly. Or maybe that's just what they wanted us to believe, because his compact car, filled with gasoline just that morning, exploded on impact and the car was engulfed in such huge flames the Good Samaritans who stopped to help couldn't get him out. One kind soul spent the rest of his life with burn scars on his right arm and hand after reaching into the inferno in an attempt to open the passenger door. By the time the fire department got there, the blaze had finished its work. After the little Comet smoldered for three hours the firemen swept up the little pile of ashes that was all that was left of my father and put him into a plastic bag.

I will never forget that Saturday night. Our babysitter called my mother to tell her she had just passed a horrible accident and the car looked like my father's. I would learn later that because the car was so badly charred the license plate had actually melted, and it took hours for the police to make out the numbers and give my mother the bad news. In the meantime, we waited. My grandparents came over. Aunts and uncles came over. The pastor came over. I remember my Jewish grandmother and my mother sitting on the couch nestled together under a red and black afghan next to the crackling fire beneath the white mantel, and they were screaming over and over, "Not Bill, not Bill, please God, not Bill." They were hoping against hope that he had taken the back roads and had car trouble or a flat tire, and would soon walk into the living room wondering why everyone was crying. Nobody sat in his rocking chair. As my mother and grandmother wailed and the houseful of people stared in stunned silence, awaiting the county sheriff's knock on the door with the news that Saturday night, I slid across the slick varnish of the new oak floors in my one-piece pajamas. I remember, as I glided past the front door, my grandfather, a handsome Austrian man, was standing there in the little alcove, head bowed, and he placed his hand on my shoulder and with a look of calm despair said, "Son, not now."

Strangely, I don't remember the days or years after that Saturday night in 1961. In all of the pictures taken of me in my early childhood, I'm holding a gray bunny rabbit. Every single picture. Maybe it had become my security; I'm not really sure.

My mother, having no formal education, could only find work making hot dogs at the Soquel Avenue Carwash in Santa Cruz, California. The redbrick fireplace and the house surrounding it, along with the four other houses still under construction, sold quickly to another builder. My mother used the little profit to purchase a double-wide mobile home in Soquel, fourteen miles away from that house and that awful Saturday night memory. My grandparents were the glue that held us together during those first few years. They brought us groceries and took care of my sister and me while my mother struggled to live, taking a few secretarial classes and sinking deeper into anger and depression. But I don't remember any of this. Actually, between Saturday, December 23, 1961, and a painful Saturday in 1966, I don't remember much of anything.

The Day I Awoke

I finally came out of that haze when I was eight years old. The moment when the veil was lifted is carved in my memory. It was the first day we moved from the trailer park into a house made of wood. It was a California tract home with 1,128 square feet and three bedrooms. It even had a white mantel over a redbrick fireplace. We put the clock on it and placed my father's rocking chair in front of the fireplace, and I thought I was safe and secure once again. That Saturday morning, my grandfather brought over a brand-new Sears and Roebuck push lawn mower and gave me instructions on how to use it. Sometime in the afternoon I went out to the garage, which was filled with moving boxes, our blue Dodge Dart, and the Sears and Roebuck mower. I remember standing in the garage and looking out at the tract homes all in perfect symmetry under a blue California sky and thinking to myself, *I'm home and I want to stay right here for the rest of my life.*

I was so proud to make my mother's yard beautiful, just like the rest of the neighbors' manicured lawns, and I would mow that lawn every week for the next fourteen years of my life. I believed this little cracker-box neighborhood where every house looked exactly the same (once I was playing outside with a friend and he went home to the wrong house) was the most exclusive community the world had to offer. One neighbor even had a swimming pool.

I vividly remember the day because it was the first time I can recall my mother swearing at me. On that first day as my mother's landscaper, I stood on the front step with her, proudly looking on the freshly cut grass, when she saw something that disturbed her. She suddenly grabbed me by my ear and pulled me over to the center of the lawn, just above the crown where it sloped off down to the sidewalk below. There, to her horror and my surprise, was a three-inch by two-foot sliver of lawn I had missed. Suddenly, before my eight-year-old eyes, my mother's face contorted and twisted as if manipulated by some kind of tyrannical metamorphosis. First she blamed me for being lazy, and then said something about me never amounting to anything in this life, and as she stormed back to the front door, leaving me standing over my failure in shame as other neighbors quietly manicuring their hedges with handheld clippers looked on in amazement, she turned toward me once again. I thought this was a dream and I would wake up to hear her say, "Great job, son." But instead, in that split second my childhood innocence was shattered when, coming out of her mouth, I heard the words, "You little son-of-a-b—h! You can't do anything right. You're good for nothing and from now on I'll just have to mow the lawn myself! You're nothing but a G—d d—n son-of-a-b—h!"

That's the day I woke up. And it always puzzled me why her favorite name for me, used over and over again, year after year, was "son-of-a-b—h." Since I was her son, and she my mother.

That Saturday began the long nightmare, as I realized my sister, Kathy, and I were being raised by a mentally, physically, and verbally abusive mother. Kathy and I would later learn my mom suffered from Borderline Personality Disorder. At ten years old my sister became my mother's caregiver. She cleaned the house and cooked most of our meals. You can't make too many mistakes living on Campbell's tomato soup and Ritz crackers. In public, my mother was high-functioning and could mask her severe mental disorders well. Our church once crowned her Mother of the Year. But in our home, she cast the veil aside.

Every Other Saturday

Saturdays were the worst. For some reason, every other Saturday something clicked within my mother's psyche and she would spiral down into chasms and canyons of uncontrollable wrath. Maybe she just needed to blow off some steam. She would often tell us that our performance of cooking, cleaning, and land-scaping was subpar at best. And, unfortunately, she really had no alternative this Saturday than to commit suicide. She would stomp out past the white mantel surrounding the redbrick fire-place and slam the door, which for some reason always made the alarm in the antique mantel clock chime. Right before the thud of the door and the sound of the alarm, she would always yell something about us never seeing her again. Some Saturdays Kathy and I secretly wished she was telling the truth. But, of course, we would follow her out to the car, begging that she wouldn't kill herself, because we already felt enough shame as it was and we didn't want to be blamed for her death by all the neighbors who were listening as they quietly trimmed their hedges. And then she would pull the car out of our garage and drive like—and these were her words—"a bat out of hell" down our block. I would actually describe her driving through our neighborhood as a crazed maniac, but "bat out of hell" seems appropriate too.

A 1963 Dodge Dart and Lawrence's Accordion

For whatever reason, she always outlined the same suicide plan: driving over the cliffs a few miles away, into the Pacific Ocean. I would picture her 1963 Dodge Dart leaping over the cliff at Steamer

Lane or Thirteenth Avenue Beach on West Cliff Drive, kicking up dust as the two back tires skidded off the gravel on the edge of the embankment and gliding awe-inspiringly into the sea. Once she told us she was going to take us with her and we'd all die together in the ocean. I thought, with all the ways you could kill yourself, this had to be one of the more awesome ways to go. I thought about her plunging into the Pacific and looking out her windows to see the confusion of the otters and sea lions who'd never seen a blue Dodge Dart as she slowly drifted like Disneyland's "It's a Small World" to the bottom of Monterey Bay, a Jacques Cousteau–esque moment of glory.

I was always puzzled how a person could be so crazy and yet so mindfully creative, almost artful, in their manipulative abilities. She was a master at stealing the innocence of my sister and me, leaving us to wonder every other Saturday if the next adult to walk through that front door would be the local sheriff bearing the bad news that our dearest mother had driven from here to eternity in a '63 Dodge Dart over the cliff at the Thirteenth Avenue Beach, and the brave surfers had fought off the curious sea lions and rescued her out of the sinking car but it was too late and he was going to have to take us to juvenile hall where they had no rocking chairs or white mantels or redbrick fireplaces and where everyone ate Campbell's tomato soup all the time.

But my mother always came back. She came back late every other Saturday night after our tomato soup and Ritz crackers and Jackie Gleason and *The Lawrence Welk Show*, where the bubbles behind Lawrence playing his accordion on Saturday nights always let me know life was better—no, *I* was better—than I was being told. My favorite part of *The Lawrence Welk Show* was the finale: "Good night. Sleep tight and pleasant dreams to you. There's a wish and a prayer that every dream comes true. And now till we meet again, adios, au revoir, auf wiedersehen." And then Lawrence would close the show with those bubbles, and every Saturday night

he would say, "Until we meet again, keep a song in your heart."
I loved that show.

Campbell's Tomato Soup

After she came home late every other Saturday, my mother would
go straight into her bedroom, slam the door, and close us off from
her surreal world. Kathy and I would sit outside her door, and my
sister, who is much more clever than I, would say with a quiver,
"Mommy, I have some tomato soup for you and it's still warm on
the stove. Would you like some?" I think my sister thought she
could lure her into our waiting arms of affection with Campbell's
soup. The response from the other side of that door was always
the same: "As far as I'm concerned, you can both go to hell." And
for some strange reason, I always tried to make myself believe she
wanted us to go to hell not because she didn't love us but because
she hated tomato soup as much as I did. For whatever reason, I
couldn't endure the taste of tomato soup for years.

For all the years of our youth, my sister and I remained bewil-
dered and ashamed of our mother's behavior. Family members, my
grandmother mainly, tried desperately to help her, but my mother's
response was always to rail against anyone who even hinted that
she might need help. Years later, after my sister was married and
had her own children and threatened to never see her again unless
she got help, my mother finally agreed to see a church counselor,
and as he got closer to making her face her own truth, my mother
would come home seething out expletives about his qualifications
and character, and sometimes even his manhood.

In our teenage years, her inner fury became more explosive,
more than just every other Saturday. She injured a disk in her
back and the doctor prescribed pain pills, to which she quickly
became addicted. Her physical violence toward us escalated, and
I remember one Saturday when Kathy became her punching bag.

It's still so clear: Kathy was five minutes late coming home from a date with a good kid from the church youth group, and the next thing I know my mother is straddling my sister, pinning her to the floor, and screaming out words that a crowned "Mother of the Year" should never say, with that metamorphous-contortion thing going on in her countenance. And I don't want to get involved because I'm right in the middle of watching a very funny comedy sketch on *The Carol Burnett Show*, and I know if I interfere things will get much worse and she'll take flight out the door threatening something about the Thirteenth Avenue Beach and Jacques Cousteau and a journey to the bottom of the sea, and screech like a bat out of h-e-double-toothpicks down our street in her '63 Dodge Dart and it's already past ten and the bubbles behind Lawrence had floated around two hours ago already and there's no one left to say to me "Good night, sleep tight, and pleasant dreams to you; there's a wish and a prayer that every dream comes true," so I would rather keep quiet and mind my own business, thank you very much.

But right before the punch line of a Tim Conway and Harvey Korman parody, the blows started flying and I knew I was going to miss the rest of the show. I got up from the couch, and it took all of my strength to pull my five-foot-four-inch mother off of Kathy as she mercilessly continued beating her in front of the redbrick fireplace and white mantel with the clock on top whose alarm chimed with every strike of the back of my sister's head against the oak floor.

What's troubling to me now is that the routine nature of my mother's psychotic behavior had anesthetized me from feeling my sister's pain. I had actually weighed the two choices: do nothing and enjoy Harvey Korman, or rescue Kathy and miss the show.

Escape from California

When Kathy turned eighteen she was accepted to the University of Oregon in Eugene, about a ten-hour drive away. We were preparing to leave on a Saturday morning, and it must have been one of those every other Saturdays because my mother had a total mental breakdown. I think the prospect of losing control over Kathy's life put her under. We literally carried her to the garage and laid her in the backseat of the Dodge Dart, covering her with the same red and black afghan that had sheltered her the night my father was killed. And I, Aaron Früh, a sixteen-year-old who had never been out of the state of California, drove my sister and crazy mother from the San Francisco Bay Area all the way to Eugene, Oregon, using a Rand McNally road map and tapping the pocket of my blue jeans every once in a while, just to make sure the laminated driver's license I had just gotten from the DMV was still there.

Across the many miles my mother moaned and mumbled to herself from under the afghan, and the only time we could make out what she was saying was when she called us dirty names for talking too loudly. When we crossed over the state line into the prairie land of southern Oregon, I glanced over at Kathy and I saw a half smile on her thin lips and peace on her countenance I had not witnessed before. She was finally home, and the funny thing is she's lived in Oregon ever since. I'll never forget pulling away from my sister's dorm building, looking in the rearview mirror, and seeing her smile. At last she was free and secure, safe from my mother's torment.

Two Life-Changing Realizations

During my college years I lived at home and attended a university nearby. I was accepted to a university in Seattle, Washington, but the thought of driving my mother all the way to the Puget Sound in the backseat under the afghan changed my mind. The real reason was, of course, that I didn't know how she would make the drive home alone or manage living by herself. Maybe I had Stockholm syndrome, where victims sympathize with their abusers, or maybe I just felt responsible for her.

In my young adulthood I was rescued by the love of my life, a Swedish girl and college nurse named Sharon Svensson. We married and moved to Chicago, where I attended grad school at Wheaton College. The first ten years of our relationship were horrible. I had suppressed all of the rejection and anger from my childhood, and when I got married it all came pouring out. When our first daughter, Rachel, was born I began to wonder if I would ever verbally curse her like I had been cursed.

On a ministry trip to California, I stopped to spend a few days with my mother. Sitting in the living room on a Saturday evening, watching *The Smothers Brothers Comedy Hour*, I asked my mother to tell me her story. I said I was curious why she had so much pain and if she was ever mistreated as a child, and why she had been so angry at my sister and me while we grew up. And she looked at me, and once again her face contorted, and she said, "You have no idea what you're talking about! I had wonderful parents and you had a great childhood and I never once swore at you and Kathy!" After that she unleashed a loud volley of expletives aimed at my personhood and identity, and we both turned back to the comedy show. Soon after I headed off to bed, falling asleep listening to my mother laughing hysterically at Tom and Dick Smothers' jokes.

On that trip to California I realized two things. The first was that because my mother had buried her story, she was never able to liquidate the mental real estate that had kept her bound all those years. I knew the same could be true for me. American philosopher George Santayana is noted for saying, "Those who cannot remember the past are condemned to repeat it." To avoid or sugarcoat our stories is to ensure that we're going to repeat in our futures the things that happened to us in our past. This means we really need to be honest about our stories so that we can forgive, clear out some mental baggage, and move on toward resilience. The first part of my marriage I could not or would not face the reality of my story, and as a result I was setting myself up for a major implosion of everything that was important to me.

On the plane home to Chicago after that conversation with my mother, I realized the second thing: I knew that I desperately needed help to find out who I was *really*, where I had come from, and where on earth I was going. I knew I wasn't going to bounce back until I could liquidate the painful mental real estate that had me bound. After returning home I called a Christian counselor I had graduated with from Wheaton. She was safe but also extremely honest, and I trusted her. Over the next two years I went on a journey of discovery. God healed my mind, restored our marriage, and released me from unforgiveness toward my mother. In the process I also helped Kathy, who at that time had been estranged from our mother for five years, to find her way back home.

The Note on the Back of a Picture

My mother passed away in 2006 from stroke-induced dementia. As she declined, she had lucid moments where she had total recall of things that happened decades before. On one Saturday afternoon, as I was sitting on the edge of her bed, she looked up at me and asked me if I would forgive her for despising me so deeply. I assured her I had forgiven her years before, and then she told me what my sister and I had long suspected from things we would hear her say beneath her breath when we were kids. When she was twenty-one, before coming to faith and meeting my father, she got pregnant and drove across the border into Mexico for an abortion. After she told me her story, I asked if the baby was a boy, and she began to sob uncontrollably. She said, "Aaron, yes, it was a boy, and every day I look at you reminds me of my shame." Then I realized why my mother continually cursed me: by cursing me she was cursing herself. A few days before my mother passed away, I walked into her apartment at the memory care center Kathy had arranged for her, not far from Kathy's home in the Columbia River Gorge in Oregon, to find my sister brushing my mother's hair and singing to her, still trying to lure my mother into her waiting arms of affection and love.

When my sister and I cleaned out our mother's house, we found a picture from Mom's eighth grade graduation, and on the back she had written:

> Nora, 1939. Taken at Aunt Lennie's home. They bought my clothes and Aunt Lennie fixed my hair. She cared and did for me what couldn't or wouldn't have been done. When I look at this picture I feel sad and wish to rescue her from that terrible loneliness and rejection, void of love, that is coming and already is.

When we read the note we realized once again why, despite her psychotic and cruel behavior, we felt, as adults, so much empathy for our mother.

The Menu at Kathy's Restaurant

My mother's funeral was a day of poetic justice, reckoning, and restoration. The poetic justice came because my mother was a Rush Limbaugh–loving ultra-conservative Republican and Kathy was and is an ultra-left-leaning Democrat. Kathy climbed the ranks in the Democratic Party in Oregon, serving as press secretary for the state senate Democrats, and in several cabinet-level agencies for two Democratic governors. She finished her journalistic career as the editor of *Oregon Business Magazine* before moving up to the Columbia River Gorge to fulfill her lifelong dream of owning a restaurant. All those years of cooking for us inspired her to want more from the food world than Campbell's tomato soup.

Most of my mother's rage toward Kathy over the last several years of her life was because of Kathy's political views. From the funeral home to the cemetery, my journalist brother-in-law, Stu, led the way in his Subaru Outback with a windsurfing board on the top rack and a bumper sticker that read, "Impeach Bush," the hearse trailing behind. The irony of my mother being led to her final resting place by a far-left banner inspired by political viewpoints that caused her so much anger toward my sister was to me more comic than tragic—a kind of poetic justice. I sat in a rented minivan with my Swedish wife and our four kids, winding along the Columbia River, the morning sun slipping through the trees, and smiled, thinking of my mother who despite her mental illness had a funny sense of humor, now healed and in her right mind, looking down from heaven and seeing the surfboard and the bumper sticker and smiling too.

The reckoning part of my mother's funeral came at the graveside, when three of my father's Jewish sisters stood with Kathy and me around my mother's casket. Pitted against each other by my mother—a trait of her borderline personality—we had all heard derogatory comments about each other, and at all times one of us would be her confidant until that one confronted her with truth. It was an endless cycle of on-again, off-again relationships. And as we all stood there, we began telling each other we were sorry for believing the things she had said about the others. We all spoke words of forgiveness to one another and even talked to the casket—strange but freeing—and forgave my mother as well.

The restoration came at dinnertime that night, sitting in Kathy's restaurant, a fine dining venue that had received rave reviews throughout the greater Portland area. (Later that year, my sister would open a second restaurant and name it Nora's Table. She said she wanted to hear our mother's name and have positive thoughts attached to it, and that restaurant, too, became a draw for many miles around. Now, that in itself is a testament to the power of bouncing back!) Sitting there at Kathy's first restaurant that day with my family, Kathy's family, my aunts, and my cousins, and

reading the menu selections, an item in the appetizer section released a taste bud I hadn't savored since I was a kid, and when the
waitress took my order I said, "I'll have the tomato soup, please."
And it was delicious and it was Saturday.

Forgive for Giving

They say when God does a work of healing in your life it's like
peeling an onion: one layer at a time. After my mother's death I
really felt my story was complete. First there had been pain and
now, after facing it, my life would be pleasurable. But there was
another layer to be peeled away, and more remained, still. What
happened next in my journey to resilience was the most difficult
part of the passage.

You see, I had forgiven my mother and was living free from
resentment toward her or anyone else: triumph! But what I didn't
recognize was that although I had forgiven my mother I had not
forgiven God for giving me to her; I had not forgiven for giving.
Which really doesn't make any sense because you can't forgive
God; He is perfect and has never done anything to you that would
require your forgiveness. But I didn't know that then, and so I had
resented Him, just under the surface of my faith, since childhood.
I was offended because I lost the security of my father's love and
along with it the rocking chair and white mantel and redbrick
fireplace and oak floors and ticking clock. I was offended at God
for giving me to my mother to bear.

Not Your Garden-Variety Kind of Weeping

What I could never figure out was why, since early adulthood, I had
moved from house to house every few years, buying and selling,
making a profit and reinvesting in the next house. I thought it was
just a hobby, but looking back now I see it was a futile attempt

to build my own fortress of security. I kept moving because I was longing for a redbrick fireplace with a white mantel, but in every house I bought (eleven in all) something was off. The first had a white mantel but white marble surrounded the firebox. The second had red brick but no mantel at all. The third had a mantelpiece and brown brick. Not one of the eleven houses had the right combination I was longing for. With each move I was trying to duplicate the security I felt God had taken from me when I was three.

Along with every house purchase, I was acquiring the mental real estate of self-sufficiency. It was expanding into a significant landmass in my heart that I needed to liquidate but I didn't know how. Then God, in His loving mercy, challenged my mind by peeling back that layer of self-reliance and revealing the resentment that was in my heart.

My daughter Hannah wanted to attend a private high school for her junior and senior years, and we lived about thirty miles away at the time, so I bought a fixer-upper a few blocks from the school. We rehabbed the property, rented out our furnished home, and lived by the high school for the next two years. After Hannah graduated, we put that house up for sale and moved back.

I had been on a roll for twenty-five years, buying and selling properties and doing really well, but that house did not move. Over the course of a year we had three offers, but each one fell through. During that time period we were paying two mortgages and were coming to the breaking point financially. The regret and shame I was experiencing were deep and biting. The four roadblocks—self-pity, disappointment, resentment toward God, and indecisiveness—had me in their grip. I had come to a complete standstill both spiritually and emotionally.

Finally, after a year and a half, we received a solid, full-price offer! A few weeks before the closing date I was in the house by myself, packing boxes and thinking how I had just dodged a bullet. I also thought about what I was going to do with the profit, how I was a winner once again, that I wasn't going to be in the foreclosure lines with all the other people who weren't as smart as I was, what a wise decision I had made to buy this house in the first place, and how I could take care of myself better than God Himself. But as "isn't life amazing" endorphins cascaded up and down and all around my veins and arteries like a Starbucks double macchiato espresso, my cell phone rang—and the Realtor said the couple that bought my house had found a brand-new home they liked better, and would I be so kind as to drop by the office and sign some papers to end the contract?

I stood in the front doorway, and the best way I can explain what happened next is that every circuit in my central nervous system had the electricity blown out of it. I walked toward the couch but before I could reach it I hit my knees and fell face-down on the living room floor, in front of the gray stone mantel with white marble surrounding the firebox, and I wept. It wasn't just any garden-variety kind of weeping either. It was a double-clutched, pedal to the metal, all-out wail. And, in that moment, the living, resurrected Lord Jesus, in one breathtaking sixty-second, Steve McQueen–kind of flying hurl down Lombard Street in San Francisco, liquidated the mental real estate that had held me back since childhood: shame, self-sufficiency, pride, and unbelief were gone. At the same moment the road-blocks of self-pity, disappointment, resentment toward God, and indecisiveness, which had been built on that now-liquidated landmass, were gone too.

As I lay there weeping, I heard myself saying over and over again, "I love You, God. I trust You, God. I love You, God. I trust You, God." Wave after wave of God's love flowed over me, and for the first time since I was three years old I climbed up into a Father's waiting arms. And for once in my life I didn't need a white mantel, a redbrick fireplace, freshly varnished oak floors, or a ticking clock, because I had Him. He was all I would ever need and He was good.

When I got up from the floor, the salt from my tears still moist on my lips, I walked over to my desk by the window in the living room, the blue Alabama sky pouring in through the French doors and the bright yellow drapes. I sat down, pulled out a piece of paper, took a pen from the drawer, and wrote down the word *bounce* and the first rough-draft outline of this book.

BOUNCE TAKEAWAY:
Reflect on Your Own Story

1. As you look at the story of your life is there one thing—a painful thorn—you would like to experience as a blessing? What is that one thing?

2. As you think about resilience, what are some mental real estate holdings—mind-sets—that you would like to liquidate? You can list them in your bounce journal under the heading: "Mental Real Estate to Be Liquidated."

3. What do you think would be a benefit of writing and sharing your life story? What would be the risk? Do you think it's worth the risk to be vulnerable and share your story?

BOUNCE CHALLENGE #9

Write your story in all of its beauty and ugliness and then share it with at least two people, because it's worth the risk. In your bounce journal, I would encourage you to write the first entry to your life story. Start with the most painful event that ever happened in your life. This may take you a few days and several pages. The best way to get started is to simply put your pen to the page of your journal and let the pen take flight. Don't stop to correct grammar, punctuation, or spelling. Just write as the words flow from your memory. If you are uncomfortable writing, you may want to speak your story into a recorder and then transcribe it on paper later. The form doesn't matter.

As you write, you may see your own story clearly for the first time. I pray that you will see beyond your own limited view and find God's hand in even the most difficult circumstances. When that happens, and I know it will, describe how our vulnerable God who suffers with us is turning your ash heap into something remarkably beautiful.

10

Embrace Perplexity

I had power over nothing. And that's when this feeling
came over me like a warm blanket. I knew, somehow,
that I had to stay alive. I had to keep breathing even
though there was no reason to hope. And all my logic
said that I would never see this place again. So that's
what I did. I stayed alive. I kept breathing. And one day
my logic was proven all wrong because the tide came
in, and gave me a sail. And now, here I am. I'm back in
Memphis, talking to you. I have ice in my glass. And I
know what I have to do now. I have to keep breathing.
And tomorrow the sun will rise, and who knows what
the tide will bring in.

Tom Hanks, *Castaway*

We both sat motionless as we stared at the computer screen
like two deer on the back roads of Wisconsin staring into
the bright headlights of an oncoming eighteen-wheeler. My musi-
cian friend Steve and his family had taken shelter in our church

in Mobile, Alabama, with my wife and kids and a lot of other people to ride out Hurricane Katrina. It was late in the evening, August 28, 2005. Steve was sitting at my desk with me and we had just pulled up the National Oceanic and Atmospheric Administration (NOAA) website to monitor the wind speed and trajectory of the storm.

When the satellite image appeared, we both looked at each other in disbelief and, without saying a word, our eyes told the tale. Katrina had shifted its path east, away from New Orleans, and was expected to make landfall somewhere between Pass Christian, Mississippi, and Pensacola, Florida. Most of the possible tracks on the screen pointed to a swath of coastline about fifty miles west of us, which sounds safe until you realize that when you're on the east side of a monster hurricane you're going to get plastered by the whip-around winds because hurricanes move counterclockwise.

As we looked at that computer screen and saw Katrina's massive strength and breadth—encompassing four states and several hundred miles of coastline along the Gulf of Mexico—our expressions said, *Dude, what have we done?* Steve and I both agreed we should have evacuated and headed to Nashville, like the wise people, but it was too late because everybody else was probably looking at NOAA too, and the television news was reporting huge traffic jams on all the northbound interstates and highways. The scenes they were broadcasting looked something like evacuees shoving and pushing their way onto the last helicopters out of Vietnam. So it was either make a break and risk facing 173-mile-per-hour winds on the open road in something like a South American soccer stampede or hunker down in a reinforced concrete church building on high ground. We stayed.

Sometime the next morning, around 3:00 a.m., the roof caps covering the parapet of our sanctuary were pried from their fasteners like someone trying to pull the yoke from the hands of a desperate pilot in an emergency free fall, and the roof membrane rolled up and sailed away somewhere, maybe to Nashville where the wise people went. The next day our team cleared the debris from around the church, surveyed the damage, and called a roofing company that immediately responded and covered the sanctuary with temporary blue tarps. For the most part, our facility had weathered the storm. The news was reporting that Gulfport, Long Beach, Pass Christian, and Bay St. Louis, Mississippi, were the hardest hit areas.

Two days after Hurricane Katrina plundered the Gulf Coast, I headed over to the epicenter with three guys from our church: Larry, his son Devon, and Fred. We loaded the back of Fred's Toyota Corolla with Meals Ready to Eat (MREs) and flat tire repair canisters in case we ran over roofing nails or other sharp objects.

White Oak Trees

The bridge on Interstate 10 near Moss Point, Mississippi, had been severely ruptured by ships—yes, ships. The ships had been pushed about ten miles inland by the twenty-seven-foot wave surge and the hurricane force winds. Now that the water had receded, it was an eerie sight to see barges and ships along a major freeway. We were forced to take the back roads to Gulfport and then turned east onto 98, the beachfront highway. Lining this quaint road along the shoreline were hundred-year-old southern mansions. We really expected to see major devastation, fallen trees, caved-in roofs, and people with chain saws cutting away limbs in order to get through their front doors. However, we saw little damage to the roofs and siding of the first row of homes facing the sea. Most of the homes were simply gone.

We pulled into one driveway and walked up to the concrete slab that had once supported a large house, and it was as if someone had taken a leaf blower and blew away every particle of white sand, perfectly clean. And then we saw the strangest thing: white oak trees. Many of the oak trees along the gulf were white, like someone had a football rally and wrapped them with toilet paper. When we got closer to the trees we realized what had happened. The winds had first blown out the windows of the coastal homes and then the roofs came off, and all the dressers, hope chests, and closets were opened. And, like a magic carpet, the bedsheets gently drifted up toward the open, whirling sky, along with the socks, underwear, white towels, kids' one-piece pajamas, and wedding dresses stored for a walk down a middle aisle one day. Bathrobes and nightgowns danced and leapt out of the open windows and, like puffy white clouds, the underwear and bedsheets floated and turned in the wind as the pounding waves washed the homes out to sea. When the eye of Katrina (the calm period of a hurricane before the second half starts to blow) was over top the foundations and surrounding oaks where the mansions used to be, the wedding dresses, along with their attendants—the towels, sheets, and nightgowns—softly floated down from the heavens like silently falling snow and decorated the oaks like white-frosted Christmas trees.

The Most Perplexing Moment Ever

We made our way through Gulfport and arrived in Long Beach. We were looking for a church or community building to set up a food distribution center. There were thousands of people out of water, electricity, and food, and many were homeless. Stores were gone, just washed away. Medical clinics, police stations, and government buildings were either destroyed or severely damaged. We found a church still standing with a dazed assistant minister inside. A section of the building's roof had been blown off, and you could look up and see open sky. However, the Sunday school and kitchen areas were still intact. We promised the young man and his wife we would be back in two days with food and water.

On the way back to Mobile, we wound our way through the back roads of Mississippi. The only way I can describe what I saw that day was that it looked like a nuclear bomb had exploded, because everything was out of place. Cars were on houses, ships and barges were on roads, trucks were up in trees, a house from two blocks over was resting upside down in someone else's backyard. When we finally got to I-10, cars lined the shoulders of the freeway for miles in both directions because the drivers, in their desperate flight from the storm, had run out of gas because they didn't have time to fill up before they left. I saw grandmas and grandpas pushing their cars down the side of the road toward the next interchange to purchase gas. But the gas stations were either destroyed or already bone dry from two nights before, in the evacuation, so these people were stranded. We pulled in behind a blue Chevy Impala with Louisiana plates and a raised hood, as the car in front of it was pulling away. The next few moments of time would be the most perplexing experience of my life, before or since.

The windows of the car were rolled down because the outside temperature was in the high 90s with 100 percent humidity. All four of us got out of Fred's car and walked up to the blue Chevy. Inside were two mothers, their mothers, and seven children. We asked if we could help in any way. The two younger moms got out of the car and told us they were fleeing from New Orleans. Their homes in the 9th Ward had been swamped when the levies broke, and they had made their escape with only the clothes they were wearing. They were headed to Atlanta, Georgia, and weren't sure how to get there because they had never in their lifetimes been out of New Orleans, and their cell phone batteries had died, and would we be so kind as to let them use ours so they could tell their uncle in Atlanta they were safe and headed north to take refuge in his home? They also told us their alternator belt had snapped and the car that had pulled out a minute before was driven by their two husbands, who were on their way to the next interchange to find an auto parts store.

On top of losing all of their belongings in the storm, they were also out of money and food. We broke out the remaining MREs and passed them to the two grandmothers and seven children who were now sitting on the grass on the side of the road. One of the grandmothers called her brother in Atlanta—only to find he had moved to Chicago.

If all of this wasn't perplexing enough, their story got even worse. We waited until after the meal was over to break the bad news to them, and Fred volunteered to deliver it to one of the grandmothers. "Ma'am," Fred said, "There is no auto parts store in the town your sons-in-law have driven to." And she said, "Well, I'm sure there is, it's a good-sized town." Fred said, "Ma'am, we just came from there, and the auto parts store is gone." And she said, "Well, maybe there's a new auto parts store in the town." Then Fred said, "Ma'am, there is no other auto parts store in the town because the town is gone—it's all gone—been destroyed by the sea and the waves, the whole town, every bit of it, ma'am."

In that moment this dear grandmother started weeping and praying, "Oh Jesus, oh Jesus, help us sweet Jesus." And we did the only thing we could do: we cried and prayed with her. As I stood there and looked east and then west and saw hundreds of cars out of gas in both directions on I-10 and heard the cries of this grandmother, I was filled with perplexity because I didn't know what to do.

And then I thought of the Scripture in Luke 21 where Jesus talked about the overwhelming perplexity of the last days of time when He said, "And there will be signs in the sun, in the moon, and in the stars; and on the earth distress of nations, with perplexity, the sea and the waves roaring" (Luke 21:25). *When Jesus said this,* I thought to myself, *surely He was looking two thousand years into the future and saw the sea and the waves roaring as the winds and gusts of Katrina churned and howled and beat down the auto parts store with the alternator belt hanging on a little hook in aisle three, the key to rescuing the blue Impala and the crying grandmother and her family.* Surely, two millennia ago Jesus looked down I-10 and saw the blue Chevy with its hood up, carrying eleven thirsty and hungry souls whose safe harbor now seemed out of reach because their uncle had moved to Chicago and they'd never been out of New Orleans so they had no comprehension of the vast space of the thousand miles between them. Surely, Jesus looked down through the scenes of time and saw four perplexed men with eleven empty MRE packages who didn't know what to do, sitting in the grass on the shoulder of that long, lonesome freeway with hundreds of stranded refugees that made it look more like a Mel Gibson Mad Max movie than anything, with an old grandmother from the 9th Ward of New Orleans who was filled with perplexity and crying out His name.

When the two men came back empty-handed from the town that was no longer there, we helped them find a junkyard where they could buy a used fan belt and gave them the address to our church, which was about fifty miles away, in case they needed shelter. And out on that melting asphalt we took up an offering from the four of us—all the cash we had, about $300—and gave it to the grandmother.

Simplifying Perplexity

After saying our goodbyes, we got back into Fred's car. I was overcome with perplexity, and I said, "What can we do to help these tens of thousands of people who are suffering?" And Fred said something to me that changed my life forever. It's one of the most brilliant and resilient statements I've ever heard and it's right up there with Matthew Lawson's "Press on regardless," Tigger's "I've got a top made out of rubber and a bottom made out of springs,"

Thomas Edison's "Thank God for tragedies because all my mistakes have burned up," Tom Arrington's "Some days you win and other days you learn," and the script on the boll weevil statue in Enterprise, Alabama.

Here is what Fred said: "When you're perplexed and don't know what to do, it's better to shoot with a rifle instead of a shotgun." I said, "Fred, explain that to me." And he said, "You know, all we've seen today is ruin and heartache, and we're tired and perplexed because the need is great and we don't know where to start. We cannot help everyone, so what if we just help one? Instead of trying to solve every problem, working kind of like a shotgun that scatters pellets in a hundred different directions, let's plan to serve these people with the precision of a rifle and just help one couple, that assistant minister and his wife in Long Beach, Mississippi, and see what God will do." And I said, "Fred, that makes a lot of sense to me." So that's what we did.

In the next three months, by making the decision to embrace the perplexity of a disastrous situation and simplify our response, Fred, Larry, Devon, and I would witness a pretty awesome miracle of God—all because we chose to own and embrace perplexity.

At Your Wit's End

What does it mean to be perplexed? The word *perplexity* or *perplexed* as used in the New Testament comes from the Greek word *aporia*, and it basically means to be at a loss of understanding. Interesting, huh, since we're talking about bouncing back from your losses? The word *perplexity* describes a person who is out of resources and ideas and doesn't know what to do. They have reached the end of their emotional and intellectual ability to craft a solution to their problems. You've perhaps used the phrase, "I'm at my wit's end." The ancient meaning of *wit* was knowledge. So, to be at your wit's end means you have come to a place in life where you have to abide in faith because your mind cannot find the answer. The phrase "wit's end" actually comes from the book of Psalms, which describes the perplexity of sailors fighting a hurricane:

> Those who go down to the sea in ships,
> Who do business on great waters,
> They see the works of the LORD,
> And His wonders in the deep.
> For He commands and raises the stormy wind,
> Which lifts up the waves of the sea.
> They mount up to the heavens,
> They go down again to the depths;
> Their soul melts because of trouble.
> They reel to and fro, and stagger like a drunken man,
> And are at their wits' end.
> Then they cry out to the LORD in their trouble,
> And He brings them out of their distresses.
> He calms the storm,
> So that its waves are still. (Ps. 107:23–29)

Playing God

Ever since my crucible experience, where I met God in the intersection of expectation and disappointment in front of the gray stone mantel and white marble fireplace surround, my theology began a transformation. Oh, it didn't change all at once, but over the next few years, fresh winds of the Holy Spirit began to complete what the Lord had started. When I liquidated the mental real estate of pride, unbelief, and self-sufficiency and moved past the four resilience blockers, I felt a new sense of extraordinary freedom. With it came a fresh and uncluttered view of God: how I related to Him and how I related to my weaknesses and issues.

The first thing that changed in my spiritual life was that I stopped trying to be God. That was a huge hurdle, believe me. The fact that I even assumed I could think like God or choose like God is remarkable, but it happened. It happened because I was not happy with God's choices or His ways of doing things. If I were God, I thought, I would have placed a nail in the road and given the Mercury Comet a flat tire so that my father would have missed the rendezvous with the drunk driver. He would have lived and sat in the rocking chair with me in his arms and I wouldn't have had to endure the loneliness of a boy without a dad. That's what I would have done if I were God. If I were God I would have healed my mother from her mental illness so that she didn't threaten suicide every other Saturday and leave me alone with Lawrence Welk and the bubbles and my sister's tomato soup. If I were God I would have removed every haunting experience of my childhood and my life would have been so much easier.

Yet what if God gave my soul to be born within the womb of a mentally tormented woman and allowed my father to leave our home exactly when he did, knowing that a drunk driver would be on the same road at the same time? And what if in both of these choices God was fulfilling His sovereign will in my life? *What if?* What if God allowed the sting and the hurt of my most perplexing (remember, to be perplexed means to not understand) life circumstances to fulfill His ultimate purpose? What if God allowed my father to be unjustly taken from me so that I could face the crucible of that resentment, find meaning in it, and one day write a book to help you bounce back from your painful losses? What if God gave me to my mother, allowed me to experience the rejection and the verbal assaults, and one day helped me find healing from transgenerational verbal abuse so that I could help others who were verbally cursed as kids? What if God allowed the man at the Pool of Bethesda that we talked about in chapter 5 to lie there in perplexity for thirty-eight years just to make a point that it was now Israel's time to cross over into a new season of fulfilled messianic prophecies? What if God allowed me to buy a house that would not sell so that He could challenge my mind in order to reveal my heart and bring me to a place of wholeness, ending the lifelong resentment I carried toward Him? *What if?*

In the midst of my game of trying to play God, I was reading Romans 9 and these words apprehended me:

> Who in the world do you think you are to second-guess God? Do you for one moment suppose any of us knows enough to call God into question? Clay doesn't talk back to the fingers that mold it, saying, "Why did you shape me like this?" Isn't it obvious that a potter has a perfect right to shape one lump of clay into a vase for holding flowers and another into a pot for cooking beans? (Rom. 9:20–21 MSG)

Claude Monet and the Blotches

After I realized I couldn't play God anymore, I began to receive a fresh perspective of God's ability to smooth out the blotches on my life's canvas. Those splattered there by drunk drivers, melted license plates, and plastic bags filled with the ashes of tender memories; those uncommonly cruel words; and those blue Dodge Darts with red and black afghans in the backseats. I began to realize God sees all those kinds of perplexing, hurtful things that don't make sense, that are blotches on the art that is my life. With the skill He gave to the great artists, such as my favorite, Claude Monet, He gently feathers them out with His brush and blends them into the portrait of a life that's uniquely mine. And in the end, when the painting is unveiled, it's beautiful to see.

I can tell you that after a lifetime of not comprehending the implications of God's love or His incomprehensible and infallible wisdom that works everything in my life out for good (see Rom.

8:28), I had come to a place where I didn't just feel shame when I made mistakes; I believed I was a mistake.

God and Hurricanes Are Much Alike

Yet after the day of my crucible, when I came to the end of my understanding and cried out to God in distress like the sailors in the hurricane in Psalm 107, it was as if the strong winds of God's Spirit began to rearrange my theology. It was a gentle breeze at first. The bedsheets were lifted from their bedposts, and then as the winds grew stronger, from the closets and drawers too. Those places where I had God neatly folded and compartmentalized began to open up, and before I knew it the old, holey socks and towels and bedsheets were dancing out the windows of my mind and I started seeing things differently. God and hurricanes are much alike: both have a way of rearranging things.

I used to be uncomfortable with perplexity, the things I didn't understand or couldn't solve. I admired dynamic Christians who seemed flawless and I emulated their ability to package God into PowerPoint illustrations: five steps to this and ten steps to that. What always puzzled me, though, was why we always had to make God seem like He was in such a hurry, in five ordered, quick steps. Why did He need to bring a person to a place of resilience instantaneously rather than over time? Yet it all seemed so logical to me, something to reach toward in my drifting lifeboat, a buoy to snag as I went by. And even though I believed in everything I was teaching others, there was something sterile and antiseptic about the whole business.

With all of this knowledge about God, there was still a curious void in my soul that wasn't being filled. Emptiness remained. I thought after figuring out God so completely and having Him boxed up so neatly I should have had it all together and be free of my weaknesses and issues and perplexing questions about elusive red bricks and missing white mantelpieces and plastic bags filled with ashes. But after God started rearranging my understanding of Him, I began to realize my biggest problem was I didn't like perplexity. I was uncomfortable not having all the answers. My theology denied me the freedom to have imperfections and issues and questions that troubled me. I wanted it all in black and white.

Becoming Comfortable with Perplexity

I used to admire clever people who had biblical answers for everything. Now I admire real people, those who don't have it all together and, like me, are just trying to breathe as they wait in hope for what the tide may bring in tomorrow. I have come to believe it is more authentically Christian—even more human—to be comfortable with perplexity.

There are two types of people in this world: the first don't know that they don't know. That was me for most of my life. I thought I knew all the answers but actually I didn't, and on top of that I didn't know that I didn't know. The second type of people are those who know they don't know. You've got to embrace perplexity to be one of those people. You've got to learn to be content not knowing. You've got to be able to accept your flaws and issues and just keep breathing. It's not a sin to be perplexed and not know what to do. The apostle Paul acknowledged this when he said, "We are hard-pressed on every side, yet not crushed; we are perplexed, but not in despair" (2 Cor. 4:8).

In other words, Paul did not allow perplexing questions and difficult issues to drag him into self-pity and disappointment with God. I so appreciate Paul's perspective on embracing perplexity and owning it. He also said:

> Therefore, in order to keep me from becoming conceited, I was given a thorn in my flesh, a messenger of Satan, to torment me. Three times

I pleaded with the Lord to take it away from me. But he said to me, "My grace is sufficient for you, for my power is made perfect in weakness." Therefore I will boast all the more gladly about my weaknesses, so that Christ's power may rest on me. That is why, for Christ's sake, I delight in weaknesses, in insults, in hardships, in persecutions, in difficulties. For when I am weak, then I am strong. (12:7–10 NIV)

For years I misinterpreted this passage of Scripture. I only saw it through the filter of my surrounding culture, which thrives on success and power. *Ah,* I thought, *I'll just endure this short season of loss and weakness and in no time I'll be powerful again, back up on top of the world!* But that's not what Paul is saying at all. Think about it: What power is there in weakness? None. There is only weakness in weakness. Paul is not enduring a temporary weakness in order to enjoy an unending strength. He's arrived at a drastic conclusion, one that I was never comfortable with. He's saying, "I've come to the place where I'm absolutely powerless, and I'm content to stay here as long as I live." Paul even stakes claim, owns up, and embraces his perplexing and pressing issue—so pressing that he earnestly prayed three times for God to take it away. He says, "I will boast all the more gladly about my weaknesses" (v. 9 NIV). Do you see it? Paul the great apostle acknowledges that he's got issues; he owns them when he says, "my weaknesses." But he chooses to embrace them and just keeps loving and serving Jesus despite them.

In the end, Paul acknowledges his weakness is actually a gift because God's awesome power is able to make something beautiful out of the perplexing problem he cannot solve.

Is Everything That Happens to Me a Gift?

When I came to embrace perplexity as an ongoing part of life, that decision released me into the wide-open space of accepting everything that happens in my life as a gift from God. Does this mean that when the sheriff knocks on your door to tell you your father has just been burned up in a Mercury Comet you should receive this news as a gift from God? Does it mean cancer is a gift from God? Bankruptcy? Divorce? Love lost because of an affair? The death of a child? The loss of a job? The foreclosure on your home? No—God didn't force a funnel full of bourbon down the throat of the drunk man who killed my father. He doesn't send cancers, and He's the architect of marriage so He would never cause divorce.

So how can I say that loss is a gift from God? Because of what Joseph said to his brothers: "But as for you, you meant evil against me; but God meant it for good, in order to bring it about as it is this day, to save many people alive" (Gen. 50:20). And also because of what wise Solomon said: "He has made everything beautiful in its time" (Eccles. 3:11). I love the word *everything* in that verse. This means that everything that ever happens to you—everything—in time will be made into something beautiful, even though you may not understand how when the thorn of loss is causing every fiber in your being to grieve.

Is it true? Can God actually make a tragedy into a gift? What can He do with a plastic bag filled with a father's ashes? How does He turn something like that into a gift? I asked God that question for many years, and then one day I was reading Isaiah and these words lifted off the page and answered my perplexing dilemma: "to console those who mourn in Zion, to give them beauty for ashes" (Isa. 61:3). I knew then that God could turn my perplexity into a promise if I would trust Him.

So now I embrace my weakness, those perplexing questions and issues I don't have answers for, and God takes the thing—the thorn in my flesh—and turns it into something unimaginably beautiful and fulfilling. And then He pulls back another layer of the onion, and He and I start all over again working out another flaw or chink in my armor or buried, painful memory that still needs healing. I'm content with ongoing weakness and perplexity because if I still have thorns in my flesh, those things that sting, it means I'm still breathing and have a reason for being. Remember what Steinbeck wrote? "To be alive is to have scars." Bouncing back is not an easy journey. But if you're willing to liquidate the painful mental scar tissue of your past —that unmarketable real estate that's been used as a toxic waste dump—and if you can embrace your perplexity and move forward without having all the answers, you've taken two significant steps toward resilience.

Katrina: The Rest of the Story

There is no doubt hurricanes cause despair. The day I met that family in the blue Chevy Impala, I was at my wit's end, not knowing how to help in a catastrophe so complete and total. I was at the brink of despair until Fred said what he did about simplifying our mission and helping one man and his wife in the little church in Long Beach. Two days later, we stayed true to our word and headed back to the disaster zone with two twenty-four-foot rental trucks filled with food and water, donations from our church family.

With us in the caravan were volunteers from Saint Paul's Episcopal Church in Mobile. They had also rented two trucks and loaded them with relief supplies. When we arrived in Long Beach, the pastor, Jay, was waiting for us in the parking lot. Flyers had been passed out in the community, and only a few hours after we unloaded the trucks we ran out of food because several hundred people came to the church to receive help. We came back the next day with the same four trucks, and the day after that, and every day for the next two weeks.

The Start of the Medical Clinic

In the first day's supply run we also loaded a borrowed hospital exam table and a good-sized tent we had rented. I had received a call from the Rotary Club and they asked me if we could use the services of a retired doctor and a nurse practitioner. I said "certainly," not really understanding the extent of what was needed to help people medically. Dr. Dale and Nurse Dorothy drove down from Knoxville, Tennessee, and were already at the church the first day we arrived with supplies. We set up the tent and the exam table, and Dale and Dorothy made an appointment with the Mississippi Board of Health to receive their guidelines for emergency medicine and their procedures for reporting patient histories. A friend of mine from Goldman Sachs in New York wired our church the needed funds to expand the project. The first thing we did was buy a thirty-foot trailer for Dale and Dorothy to set up their medical office. Next we purchased computers to upload patient histories to the board of health. On opening day this little medical clinic had three hundred patients waiting in line. Medical need was serious because the pharmacies had been destroyed or closed down so people did not have access to their diabetic medications, heart medications, and so forth. I called a pharmaceutical company and asked for help, and they sent an overnight shipment of the needed medications—free of charge.

A Most Perplexing Storm

We were progressing nicely with the clinic and the food distribution, but then two weeks later Hurricane Rita blew in and our medical tent came down. We were at a perplexing juncture. Thousands of people were depending on us and the four trucks of food were not enough to supply the need. It took several weeks for FEMA to be mobilized, and so at this point in Long Beach, Mississippi, we were one of just a few relief centers. A lot of the national news networks at this time blamed President Bush. But the catastrophe was so vast—four states were affected—that every relief agency, including FEMA and the Red Cross, were overwhelmed. It was impossible to prepare for a storm like Katrina that affected so many people. Katrina was the largest and costliest hurricane ever to hit the United States, covering an unbelievable 93,000 square miles. It was also the most catastrophic natural disaster in US history. An estimated 1,833 people died in the storm and 705 people are still missing. The storm affected fifteen million people in all. The total economic impact on just Louisiana and Mississippi exceeded $150 billion. Katrina destroyed three hundred thousand homes. If you stacked the debris left in her wake in a football field, it would reach over ten-and-a-half miles high. We were trying, in the midst of all the rubble and devastation in the epicenter, to just keep breathing.

Just Keep Breathing and See What the Tide Will Bring In

We needed more food and a bigger tent, and another exam table would be good too. So I called the Red Cross and asked the area director for help, and he said, "Aaron, you're not an official Red Cross Emergency Center." So I said, "Could you make us official?" And he said, "That's impossible." And I said, "Sir, we have one hundred volunteers from all over America living in Sunday school classrooms, and they're ready to distribute your supplies because our four trucks can't meet the need and this area is heavily populated, and if you will give these workers a chance they'll do a great job for the Red Cross, I promise." He said, "I'll drive over to see you today."

He came and saw the way Pastor Jay had organized the food distribution, and then he said, "Aaron, you are now an official Red Cross Emergency Center. Can you unload two eighteen-wheelers of canned food and fresh produce tomorrow morning at 8:00 a.m. sharp?"

Over the next three months that Red Cross director became, in the words of Forrest Gump, "My bestest of friends." He liked us so much he sent a food truck to our site with two cooks and provided our workers with three hot meals a day.

The perplexing food problem out of the way, I now went to work finding Dale and Dorothy a better medical clinic. I had heard that European Aeronautic Defense and Space Company (EADS) had built military Mobile Army Surgical Hospital (MASH) units in Germany and the company was now bidding on a US military contract to build an air force refueling plane in Mobile, so I placed a call to their Washington, DC, office and asked if they would be so kind as to send me a German-made hospital. Within a few minutes they called back and said, "Aaron, we are sending an Airbus Beluga A300–600ST cargo jet from France to Germany to pick up the MASH unit and it will be in Mississippi in twenty-four hours with five German technicians to set up your new multimillion-dollar hospital. It comes fully equipped with a surgical department, water purification plant, post-operation unit, and central air-conditioning, and what is the address of that little church in Long Beach, Mississippi, again? And, oh, by the way, this is compliments of Airbus, so have a great day and Godspeed to you, sir, Godspeed."

All in all, Pastor Jay oversaw the distribution of food to over 250,000 people with the help of over one hundred volunteers and my best friend from the Red Cross. Dr. Dale and Dorothy cared for over ten thousand patients with the help of over one hundred other doctors and nurses who flew in from as far away as San Francisco.

Another wonderful volunteer in the clinic was a retired surgeon who performed over three hundred surgical procedures in the military hospital. With the help of a retired pharmacist, the clinic distributed over $5 million worth of life-saving pharmaceuticals.

After the local hospitals and clinics came back online three months later, our work was finished. Not long afterward the relief organization Operation Blessing called and asked if I thought Dale and Dorothy would help out in the 9th Ward (where the family in the Blue Impala was from) because they planned on investing $1 million to build a clinic there. Dale and Dorothy would spend the next five years living in the trailer and taking care of the sick in New Orleans.

When you don't know what to do, just do the one thing that seems right to you—and then watch what God does. In our case, we felt led to help one man and his wife in Long Beach, Mississippi. In a perplexing situation in which we were totally powerless, we decided to just keep breathing and wake up every morning trusting God, waiting in hope for what the tide might bring in. Our resilience, our recovery from loss, always starts that way: with one step. One thing, led by God. In our case we embraced the perplexity of Katrina and helped the one couple standing right in front of us to bounce back.

■■■

What is your first step? You may be overwhelmed with perplexity and at your "wit's end" with absolutely no idea what to do next. You cannot solve all of your issues today, but you can simplify your resilience strategy by just doing one thing that makes sense, and that one thing is sometimes the most obvious thing right before your eyes. Take a few moments before moving on to the next chapter and ask God for His power to be made perfect in your weakness. Ask for His wisdom to flood your mind in the midst of your perplexity and then patiently wait for His direction. Now, place all of your trust in Him by setting aside your propensity to try to figure everything out. In a little while you'll begin to hear His still, small voice. He has already designed your bounce-back plan and all you have to do is follow Him without having to know all the answers.

I have found that as I embrace my perplexing situations with God's wisdom, the solutions He sends my way are simple rather than complex. Here's one for you: How do you feed 250,000 people, examine ten thousand patients, and run a medical clinic for five years in the 9th Ward of New Orleans with four perplexed men in a Toyota Corolla, fifty MREs in the trunk, and no knowledge of medicine? How? By just helping one person at a time.

BOUNCE TAKEAWAY:
Reflect on Your Own Story

1. What is the most perplexing thing you have ever faced?

2. Have you been at a place where you have reached the end of your emotional and intellectual ability to find a solution to a perplexing circumstance? How does this leave you feeling emotionally?

3. I said in this chapter that God and hurricanes are much alike because they have a way of rearranging things. If you are presently in the storm of your life, what things are being re-arranged by God in your values, your understanding of His ways, and in your life vision? Are you confident that when this storm is over you will have become a more authentic person?

BOUNCE CHALLENGE #10

Simplify, simplify, simplify. Face your perplexity and think about some ways you can approach a resolution. First of all, take time to pray and ask the Lord for His wisdom. Then write down a number of possible solutions in your bounce journal. You will be surprised by the different ideas God reveals to you and how the answer to the perplexing problem is within your grasp.

11

Hope

De Profundis

Because I remember, I despair. Because I remember I have the duty to reject despair.

Elie Wiesel, "Nobel Peace Prize Lecture," Dec. 11, 1986

Maafa is a Swahili word used for the years in which European slave traders plundered the tribal groups of Africa, and it means "Great Disaster."

Beginning in the early 1500s, an estimated 11.3 million slaves were transported by ship across the Atlantic in what was known as the Middle Passage in the slave industry. Slave ships refitted their hulls to carry more slaves, usually about three hundred. The lower decks had an average height of thirty inches. Men were chained together with iron shackles around their ankles and forced into the dark, claustrophobic decks that had little ventilation, no bedding, and no room to raise their heads; coffins had more space. Dysentery spread quickly. Communal bowls were used for meals and everyone ate with their bare hands, so when one became sick so did those nearby. The death rate during the Middle Passage was high. Some died of suffocation, others of dysentery, smallpox, and fever. Some even took their lives in despair. A great disaster indeed.

Because the ship captains kept good records, we know that of the men, women, and children who were taken from their homeland, separated from their families, and chained together in the depths of filthy ships filled with vomit and human feces, 1.8 million died, and afterward their bodies were cast into the deep sea. Crews reported that from Africa to the European colonies in the Caribbean and the Americas, the slave ships were followed by schools of sharks because they supplied a constant source of food to the deadly predators.

One slave ship, the *Zong*, was headed to Black River, Jamaica, in the British West Indies. After its route was miscalculated, it was nearly two weeks from port and had only four days of potable drinking water left on board. Fearing some of the slaves would die of thirst—a problem for Captain Luke Collingwood, because he was not insured for a water shortage due to poor navigation, only if a slave died of sickness—the captain ordered the crew to throw 133 live slaves overboard into the sea in order to conserve water. The year was 1781, and the *Zong* massacre would act as a rallying cry for those passionately attempting to abolish slavery in the British West Indies. The thought of 133 men and women being thrown into the depths began to turn Europeans against the terrible business of slavery.

Fifty years later, when the slaves of the West Indies were finally freed on the Island of Antigua, something remarkable happened and it has everything to do with *De Profundis*, a special prayer that promises our amazing God is listening and is with us in our loss and that His love will bring us restoration and restitution.

Out of the Depths

One of the most passionate and raw prayers in the Bible is found in Psalm 130, and this prayer even has a name: *De Profundis*, which is Latin for "out of the depths." Psalm 130 is one of the fifteen "Songs of Ascent" between Psalms 120 and 134. Worshipers sang these songs as they ascended up the Jericho Road from the lowest place on earth in the Dead Sea region, which sits 1,400 feet below sea level, to the 2,400-foot rocky peaks of Jerusalem.

There are three pictures in Psalm 130. The first is the lament of a drowning person: "Out of the depths I cry to you, O Lord! O Lord, hear my voice! Let your ears be attentive to the voice of my pleas for mercy!" (Ps. 130:1–2 ESV). The phrase "out of the depths" (*de profundis*) is often used in poetry to describe a person who is at a place of absolute hopelessness. Within biblical literature, the phrase "the depths" describes a person drowning in troubled waters. Remember, the Songs of Ascent begin at the Dead Sea, which actually is translated from the Hebrew as "sea of death." For the ancient Hebrews, the sea represented chaos and calamity. Loss has a way of giving us the sensation we are drowning. This is what the psalmist is confirming: he's in a place of emotional torment and misery. The most sincere, raw, and passionate prayers you will ever lift up to God will come from *de profundis* . . . out of the depths.

The lament that opens Psalm 130 is a complaint that carries with it a petition for justice and mercy. Our generation has lost its appreciation for lament. We've devalued lament because of a misunderstanding of our covenant relationship with God.

When my son, Nathan, was five years old, my wife and I were drinking coffee in the living room early one morning when we heard a cry coming from his bedroom. When Sharon went into his room she screamed out to me because Nathan was having a seizure. She came running down the hall carrying his twitching and flailing body with his little brown eyes rolled back in their sockets.

I ran into the kitchen to call 911, slid across the kitchen tile, and scraped my knee. The ambulance took my son to a children's hospital and I slept next to him in his room for the next five days while the pediatric neurologists treated him.

When he had his seizure, Nathan was afraid because his body was doing strange things it had never done before, so he cried out for his mother and father. It was a lament, a complaint: "Help me! Something isn't right! Come quick! I'm afraid!" And what did I do as a father? I ran across the kitchen floor and skinned my knee. In the hospital I drew closer to my son in his distress. That's what a father does because of the covenant bond he has with his child. A lament is a form of speech that releases us, even encourages us to complain about injustice and call on God to hear our cries of suffering. And what does our Father in heaven do when we raise a lament His way? He runs across the kitchen floor and skins His knee.

There are two key components of a lament and they're found right in Psalm 130:1–2. The first is *complaint*: "Out of the depths I have cried to you, O LORD!" (v. 1 ESV). The psalmist is saying, "God, I'm in the depths of despair and sorrow and I'm really hurting. I'm drowning here!" That's the complaint. The second component of a lament is a *petition*: "O Lord, hear my voice! Let your ears be attentive to the voice of my pleas for mercy!" (v. 2 ESV). The verb tense in these verses indicate the writer of the psalm has been drowning for a while so he's asking God for mercy and rescue. As I have already noted, it's not the sting of our trouble that is so painful, it's the longevity.

Lament is ultimately praise, because it proclaims that God is in the midst of the sea of death with us and can hear our cries for help as we're being swallowed up. So the most passionate prayers you will ever pray come out of the depths of your despair—*de profundis*—and these kinds of prayers are welcomed by your heavenly Father, who is willing to bleed to rescue you.

An Attentive Watchman

The second picture in Psalm 130 is of an attentive watchman on a wall: "I wait for the LORD, my soul waits, and in his word I hope; my soul waits for the Lord more than watchmen for the morning, more than watchmen for the morning" (vv. 5–6 ESV). The word *watchman* in Hebrew is *sapha*, and it means to look intently into the distance. It also carries the connotation of leaning forward to gaze at something far away. In ancient Israel, watchmen stood on the city wall, leaning forward to watch for messengers or for signs of enemy invaders. The watchmen were the first line of defense, something like the lookouts on the *Titanic* who leaned forward, peering into the darkness of the horizon, searching for icebergs. I'm sure the pressure on iceberg lookouts and on watchmen on the walls of Jerusalem was great. Miss sighting an iceberg and a ship could sink. Miss sighting an invasion and a city could be lost. I imagine those lookouts and watchmen longed for the first signs of light as they peered into the darkness during the long hours of the night, waiting for the safety of dawn.

Frederick Fleet was the first to spot the iceberg in *Titanic*'s path, at 11:40 p.m., and he rang the bell from the crow's nest three times. He survived the ship's sinking, and in the British Wreck Commissioner's Inquiry, Fleet testified that if he had been given binoculars he could have saved the ship. I think he must have lived with great shame his entire life and blamed himself for not spotting the iceberg sooner, because in 1965 Fleet committed suicide. On the one hundredth anniversary of the sinking of the *Titanic*, someone—cruelly I think—placed a pair of binoculars on Frederick Fleet's grave.

A watchman's burden was great because lives depended on him; that's why he so desperately longed for the morning. Not only did he have to keep a sharp eye out for sneak attacks but he also had to stay alert when his eyes grew heavy. The watchman knew he had no power to cause the daylight to appear yet he waited with eager expectation and absolute assurance the sun would rise.

Here in Psalm 130, the psalmist is saying that he is more desperate for God's deliverance than a watchman is eager for dawn. Employing repetition for emphasis, the writer repeats the thought twice: "My soul waits for the Lord more than watchmen for the morning, more than watchmen for the morning" (v. 6 ESV). The desperate psalmist crying out to God from the chaos of the depths of despair is saying he's at a greater advantage than the watchman because he has more assurance in the Lord's rescue than a watchman does in the sun's rising. That's serious hope!

Though filled with hope, the watchman is powerless to cause the sun to rise, yet he is assured it will. When you are crying out to God with those raw and passionate hopeful prayers from out of your depths, it means you have come to the end of yourself. You are absolutely powerless and without strength to mount a comeback. It's in this desperate place a hopeful prayer is most effective, because it starts with a complaint and ends with a petition, and the Father responds to the laments of His own children. He gets His knees all skinned up for kids like you! I love what David says in Psalm 30:5: "Weeping may endure for a night, but joy comes in the morning."

A Benevolent Relative

The third picture in Psalm 130 is of a benevolent relative: "O Israel, hope in the LORD! For with the LORD there is steadfast love, and with him is plentiful redemption. And he will redeem Israel from all his iniquities" (vv. 7–8 ESV). These two verses include two of the most important words in the Bible: *love* and *redemption*. The psalmist states, "with the LORD there is steadfast love" (v. 7). The Hebrew word for "love" here is *chesed*. Though translated as "steadfast love," *chesed* has absolutely no English equivalent because the steadfast *chesed* love of God is indefinable and unexplainable. It is a love so magnificently enduring it persists beyond our sins and failings. It is the generosity of an eternal God of wonders who chooses to be in authentic covenant relationship with His children.

In human terms, a way to describe *chesed* would be a tired and weary father driving through the night to find his runaway daughter who's called him from a city a thousand miles away wanting to come home. Or a mother sitting in a police station with a bail bondsman waiting to spring her drug addict son out of jail for the hundredth time. *Chesed* love, rather than being driven by emotion, is in essence the total expression of God's character and attributes.

John speaks of this when he says, "Behold what manner of love the Father has bestowed on us, that we should be called children of God!" (1 John 3:1). John is astonished when he comes to the realization of a love beyond comparison or comprehension, and so the only way he can sum up all the attributes of God is by saying, "God is love" (4:8).

Because lifelong love and loyalty are rare qualities these days, it's hard for us to understand God's steadfast love. God loved us while we were still sinners. He looked for us when we were not looking for Him and is faithful to us—keeping His covenant—when we are faithless toward Him. He's reliable when we're unreliable, consistent when we're not, and permanent when we're unstable and tentative. In the best but inadequate way I can explain it, that's steadfast love. *Chesed*.

The second important word found in Psalm 130:7–8 is *redeem*: "with him is plentiful redemption. And he will redeem Israel from all his iniquities." To redeem means "to buy back." There were redemption laws within the legal system of ancient Israel. If a person hit a rough patch financially, someone could buy them back from the brink of ruin by taking on the role of a kinsman-redeemer. However, they needed to meet three qualifications. First they had to be a kinsman; second, they had to be able to pay the price of redemption; and third, they had to be willing to pay the price. Wonderfully, Jesus our redeemer met all three qualifications.

The psalmist here is saying God is a close, benevolent relative who purchases the debt of a family member in need. When we, either by our own choices (those self-inflicted wounds we all make from time to time) or by unfortunate circumstances, find ourselves in a sea of chaos, we are encouraged in Psalm 130 to cry to God with a lament of praise out of the depths. *De profundis!*

Now, I'm sure you've been wondering what any of this exploration of Psalm 130 and *De Profundis* has to do with the Middle Passage and the emancipation of the slaves in the British West Indies. As it turns out, an awful lot.

The Moravians

In 1732, two young men from the Moravian church in Austria, Leonard Dober and David Nitschmann, sold themselves into slavery because a Dutch colonist had proclaimed he would never allow missionaries to proclaim the gospel to the slaves on his island, St. Thomas in the West Indies, so they became slaves themselves. Over the years the two young men established churches in St. Thomas, St. Croix, St. John's, Jamaica, Barbados, St. Kitts, and Antigua. These Moravian missionaries educated their fellow slaves and fought fiercely to end the slave trade and the merciless deaths in the depths of the Middle Passage.

After the *Zong* incident in 1781, Englishman William Wilberforce and others began to petition the government of the British Empire to end the slave trade, and in London on March 25, 1807, Parliament passed an act to end the terrible business. However, slavery in the British West Indies was still very much legal, as well as brutal. Yes, the Middle Passage, the transport of African people to the colonies, was prohibited, but the slaves of the West Indies were still living in the depths of despair.

The Moravian churches kept growing and the missionaries continued fighting to end slavery. Finally, the British government signed the Act of Emancipation and ruled that all slaves would be free in the British West Indies on August 1, 1834. However, they would have to remain enslaved for another six years of apprenticeship before they could gain complete and total freedom.

Imagine being in bondage for over three hundred years and finally gaining your emancipation—only to be ordered to remain in the shackles of bondage for six more years. On Antigua, the Moravian missionaries appealed to the governor, Mr. McGregor, and to the Antiguan legislature, asking if the slaves of Antigua could bypass the six-year apprenticeship and be free at last without further delay. Their request was granted, and as the date of August 1, 1834, approached, Psalm 130 exploded off the pages of the Bible into the lives of thirty-three thousand people.

Leaning Forward on the Island of Antigua

A prayer vigil was planned on the eve of their freedom and at 11:00 p.m. on July 31, 1834, in the little Moravian slave churches across the island of Antigua, thirty-three thousand African men, women, and children gathered to await the dawn of the next day. After three hundred years of their people being cast into the depths of the sea in the Middle Passage, like the passengers of the *Zong*, or into the depths of the bondage of slavery, they still hoped that one day their freedom would come. And what passage of Scripture did they read on the eve of liberty? What Scripture would commemorate the terror of the Middle Passage and the depth of their suffering? Psalm 130! They lit candles in those little clapboard churches, sang hymns, and read Psalm 130.

Out of the depths have I cried unto thee, O LORD.
Lord, hear my voice: let thine ears be attentive to the voice of
my supplications.
If thou, LORD, shouldest mark iniquities, O Lord, who shall
stand?
But there is forgiveness with thee, that thou mayest be feared.
I wait for the LORD, my soul doth wait, and in his word do I hope.
My soul waiteth for the Lord more than they that watch for the
morning: I say, more than they that watch for the morning.
Let Israel hope in the LORD: for with the LORD there is mercy,
and with him is plenteous redemption.
And he shall redeem Israel from all his iniquities. (Ps. 130 KJV)

Then something amazing happened. After midnight, thirty-three thousand slaves with candles in their hands climbed the mountains of Antigua. The younger men and women climbed up trees and rocky peaks and leaned forward, searching into the darkness for the first glimpse of dawn light. Thirty-three thousand people prayed Psalm 130 through the watches of that long night, lifting both the lament and the petition from the passage of Scripture, crying out to God. They looked toward the sea—for them, a sea of death—peering into the faraway distance, waiting for the Lord more than watchmen for the morning. More than watchmen for the morning.

Did they think about the *Zong* and the Middle Passage as they prayed "Out of the depths I cry to you, O LORD!"? I believe they did, and as the dawn broke upon Antigua the next morning—after waiting and watching for three hundred years—they came out of the depths. *De profundis.*

And we, who find ourselves in the depths of our own kind of despair desperately longing for restoration, vindication, and justice, wait upon the Lord in hope and solidarity with these slaves of the British West Indies. We are leaning forward and peering into the distance, awaiting the first light of the coming day of our resilience.

BOUNCE TAKEAWAY:
Reflect on Your Own Story

1. As the story of your life unfolds and you lean forward, peering into an unknown future, what are you really hoping for out there?

2. I said in this chapter that the love of God is so deep for you that it is unexplainable and indefinable. Can you recall your first encounter with God's love? What did you experience?

3. We learned that the most passionate prayers we ever pray are when we are in the depths of despair. Is it possible that one of the benefits of loss is that your prayers become more passionate and desperate? Do you see this as a blessing, and if so, why?

BOUNCE CHALLENGE #11

We discovered in this chapter that there are two key components to a lament: complaint and petition. In your bounce journal, I encourage you to write out Psalm 130 word for word. Now read this beautiful lament out loud, lifting your voice with each new verse. Remember, this is one of the Songs of Ascent the Jewish pilgrims sang as they went up to the temple, so after you have read the psalm out loud I encourage you to put a melody to the words of Psalm 130 and sing it to the Lord. If you really want to act out Psalm 130, as you sing you might even lean forward like a watchman who waits for the morning!

12

Cry Out for Justice

Dig a Hole on an Airfield before the Sun Comes Up

There may be times when we are powerless to prevent injustice, but there must never be a time when we fail to protest.

Elie Wiesel, "Nobel Peace Prize Lecture," Dec. 11, 1986

awn. Monday, May 10, 2010. The first light of the morning was slowly attempting a comeback over the waters of Mobile Bay. Seventy-five business and government leaders wove through the Mobile, Alabama, back roads of Brookley Airfield, a former air force base that was now home to several avionic companies. As the men and women walked from their cars and huddled together in the waning darkness on the edge of the runway, a few pleasant good morning greetings were expressed, but little else was said. The mood was serious, sober. The mayor of Mobile was there, along with several members of the city council and chamber of commerce.

We were there for the sole purpose of crying out to God for justice for our city. But why cry out to God on an airfield before the sun was up?

In 2008 the avionic company Airbus won a $40 billion contract with the United States Air Force to build the KC-45, a large fuel tanker airplane that could fill the bellies of fighter jets in flight. Airbus had looked at several cities to build the plane and chose Mobile because of the close proximity of Brookley Airfield to railways and waterways that would be critical in transporting the large fuselages and wings of the planes to be harnessed together in the assembly plant. For a medium-sized Southern city, you can imagine how exhilarating this news was. Other industries would come alongside the KC-45 project to provide support and this meant jobs—lots of them.

However, not long after Airbus won the bidding contract, political maneuvering and posturing prevailed and the air force awarded the prize to another great aeronautics company instead.

This was absolutely devastating news. What made it worse was that a politician who represented the other aeronautics company actually said that Alabama Southerners didn't have the intelligence to build supertankers. That hurt, because Forrest Gump is from Alabama and he's pretty smart and that's all I have to say about that.

A Decree for Justice

In January, a few months before that early morning gathering on the runway, I attended an annual business leader's prayer meeting in downtown Mobile. After the event, five businessmen asked if I would like to join them for breakfast at the Whistle Stop Café. It was a glum group. The men walked through the bidding process point by point and explained how Airbus had scored the highest on all the air force's criteria. They couldn't understand how a signed and sealed contract could just be taken away. Over the noisy clatter of silverware and the smell of hot Southern grits, Conecuh sausage, warm pancakes dripping with fresh maple syrup, and biscuits oozing with gravy, with Lucy the waitress (who has been at the Whistle Stop for as long as anyone can remember) calling us baby and honey and sugarplum every time she poured steaming coffee into our cups, I quietly said, "Why don't you write a decree for justice?"

A few weeks later I found myself standing before the key business leaders of the city in a bank boardroom in the tallest building in Alabama. Years earlier I had written a book entitled *The Decree of Esther*, and after I gave each person in the room a copy of the book I explained how a written decree is simply a petition that is written down. I described in detail from the book the power of crying out to God for justice and the value of a justice decree:

> Proverbs 8:15 says, "By me (wisdom) kings reign, and rulers decree justice." It is in our kingly roles to decree justice. . . . Oftentimes in the Scriptures God brings justice to His people through a written decree. When Nebuchadnezzar, the king of Babylon, had crushed Israel and was carrying away her people captive, God did a remarkable thing. He decreed that justice would come to His people. Jeremiah 51 is one of many prophetic decrees of justice. Even as the Jews were being led into bondage, God said, "Behold, I will plead your case and take vengeance for you" (Jer. 51:36).
>
> Jeremiah did something interesting. He took a scroll and wrote a decree concerning the just judgment that was going to come upon Babylon for her treatment of the people of God. Then he told Seraiah, one of the leaders of Israel being led away as a slave, "When you arrive in Babylon and see it, and read all these words, then you shall say, 'O LORD, You have spoken against this place to cut it off, so that none shall remain in it, neither man nor beast, but it shall be

desolate forever.' Now it shall be, when you have finished reading this book, that you shall tie a stone to it and throw it out into the Euphrates. Then you shall say, 'Thus Babylon shall sink and not rise from the catastrophe that I will bring upon her'" (vv. 61–64).

Speaking through the prophet Isaiah, God said that He would dry up the rivers of Babylon and make the crooked places straight (see Isa. 44:27; 45:2). When Cyrus the Great laid siege to Babylon, his engineers rerouted the Euphrates River by straightening it and directing it away from the city. They captured Babylon by marching on the dry riverbed underneath the city wall, thus walking directly on top of the decree that Jeremiah had written seventy years before and that now lay on the bottom of the Euphrates with a rock tied around it.[1]

Over the next few months these business leaders took to heart the words of Proverbs 8:15, "By me (wisdom) kings reign, and rulers decree justice." We met together every Wednesday morning and gradually penned a beautiful decree for God's justice in the matter of the lost Airbus contract. At that early morning gathering on the airfield, we lifted up our voices in a cry for mercy. Someone suggested we bury the decree like Jeremiah buried his decree in the Euphrates River. The mayor of Mobile dug a hole on the edge of the runway, and after placing our decree in a canister we dropped it into the hole, covered it, and quietly went back to our cars just as the sun was rising.

Let me show you how crying out for justice is a critical element in your resilience plan.

Justice Is Just Who God Is

The prophet Isaiah tells us, "No one calls for justice, nor does any plead for truth. . . . Justice is turned back, and righteousness stands afar off; for truth is fallen in the street, and equity cannot enter" (Isa. 59:4, 14). Isaiah is saying that for some reason when people suffer injustice they don't cry out to God for vindication: "No one calls for justice." Why? Perhaps it was because of a misunderstanding of the character of God. Yet justice is at the very core of God's personality and nature. One of the Hebrew names for God is *Elohei Mishpat*, which means "God of Justice." This wonderful and powerful name is also found in the book of Isaiah: "For the LORD is a God of justice (*Elohei Mishpat*); blessed are all those who wait for Him" (30:18). God's very name means justice.

When you suffer financial loss, broken family relationships, lost inheritance, health issues, ongoing financial insecurity, people taking advantage of your good nature and generosity, injustice in your business, or wounds inflicted by a person with evil intent, you can slowly allow the roadblocks of self-pity, disappointment, resentment toward God, and indecisiveness to become strongholds in your mind. You may begin to wonder, *If God is just, why am I suffering injustice?* The more pressing question you might be asking is, *If God is just, when is He going to vindicate me?* When your vindication, restoration, and restitution are delayed, you can begin to wonder if God is really just after all. I've said it before: it's not the sting of loss that is so painful; it's the longevity of the thing.

I shared with you my story in chapter 9 about my crucible moment when my house did not sell. Facing serious financial loss, I fell on my living room floor and cried out to God. You were probably thinking that at that moment my cell phone rang again and the realtor on the other end of the line was excitedly telling me the deal was still on. That, in fact, the buyer was sending a gift card from Ruth's Chris Steak House by courier that moment for all the pain he had just put me through! Well, nothing like that happened on that day four years ago. And you know what? I still have not sold that house. Instead, I embraced my perplexing situation and simplified my approach to solving the problem, asked God for wisdom, started hoping again like the slaves of the British West

Indies, and soon after, a friend traveled all the way from another country to encourage me. In our few days of fellowship my friend said to me, "Why don't you just lease the house?" I had not considered that option. And that is what I did.

So, like you, I am on this journey toward complete restoration and restitution, and as I'm waiting God is doing something wonderful on the inside of my soul. I would not trade this experience for anything! I think the most important thing I have learned in the process is to wholeheartedly trust in *Elohei Mishpat*—the God of Justice. I have come to know that God will always, in every circumstance, do the right thing on my behalf, because that's just who He is.

When it comes to crying out for God's justice, Psalm 97 offers the wounded and searching soul great comfort: "Righteousness and justice are the foundation of His throne" (v. 2). What the psalmist is saying is, "If God is not just—if He does not restore all of your losses—then His very throne has crumbled in ruins." The foundation of the throne of God, made with righteousness and justice, will never be in jeopardy.

Your Vindication Is Coming

In one of the last scenes of his vision of heaven, the apostle John sees something incredible: the throne of God still standing secure after being challenged by the adversary for centuries. "And there shall be no more curse, but the throne of God and of the Lamb shall be in it, and His servants shall serve Him" (Rev. 22:3). How can I be so sure your vindication is coming? The throne of God is established forever and justice is the foundation of His throne.

A young Scottish pastor who was struggling in his faith visited an elderly woman from his congregation who was near death. When he walked into her room, he was overwhelmed with the peace and joy that shone from her countenance. He was not intrigued by her calm assurance but rather irritated. "How can you be so certain," he said, "that you will immediately be in the presence of the Lord when you die?"

The response of this elderly saint will encourage anyone who doubts in God's ultimate justice and vindication: "If I should awake in eternity to find myself among the lost, the Lord would lose more than I would; for all that I would lose would be my immortal soul, but He would have lost His good name."

Elohei Mishpat is His name, and He stands behind it!

One of the most dramatic statements about God's justice is found in Jesus's parable of the widow who cried out to the unjust judge:

> Then He spoke a parable to them, that men always ought to pray and not lose heart, saying, "There was in a certain city a judge who did not fear God nor regard man. Now there was a widow in that city; and she came to him, saying, 'Get justice for me from my adversary.' And he would not for a while; but afterward he said within himself, 'Though I do not fear God nor regard man, yet because this widow troubles me I will avenge her, lest by her continual coming she weary me.'" Then the Lord said, "Hear what the unjust judge said. And shall God not avenge His own elect who cry out day and night to Him, though He bears long with them? I tell you that He will avenge them speedily. Nevertheless, when the Son of Man comes, will He really find faith on the earth?" (Luke 18:1–8)

Don't Be Afraid to Cry Out

The entire idea of crying out to God for justice may seem a little strange. However, Jesus sets the precedent in this passage that crying out is not only reasonable but necessary in your resilience plan: "And shall God not avenge His own elect who cry out day and night to Him, though He bears long with them?" (v. 7).

Where did we lose the concept of crying out to God for justice? As the early church grew and expanded across Europe, Greek philosophy began to infringe upon Hebraic thought. The Hellenistic idea of dualism divided a person into two parts, spiritual and physical. Spirituality was somehow divorced from the physical world; eventually dualism gave way to asceticism and monasticism, and prayer became contemplative, nonverbal, nonphysical, and intellectual. But in Hebraic biblical thought a person was one—body, soul, and spirit—and so prayer involved the whole person. Prayer was physical. The Jews lifted their voices, clapped their hands in praise, stood, laid on the ground, and cried out for justice. Prayer also involved the soul, because for the Hebrews prayer was not only intellectual but emotional. The spirit was not left out because prayer was meant to flow out of the faith in one's heart.

Jesus prayed like a Hebrew rather than a Hellenist. In the garden of Gethsemane, the night before His crucifixion, His prayer was physical because he fell on His face and sweat drops of blood. His prayer involved the emotions of His soul because He said to His disciples, "My soul is exceedingly sorrowful, even to death" (Matt. 26:38). And His prayer came from the depths of His Spirit because the Scripture says He, "in the days of His flesh, when He had offered up prayers and supplications, with vehement cries and tears to Him who was able to save Him from death . . . was heard because of His godly fear" (Heb. 5:7).

Why did Jesus the Son of God find it necessary to cry out to God? Because He knew that a cry for justice always gets God's attention. You see this throughout the history of the Jewish people. When God's people cried out in desperation, He set the course for their deliverance . . . not just once or twice but time and time again throughout the Bible. All the way back in the book of Exodus, after suffering four hundred years of slavery, the Jews cried out to God for help: "Then the children of Israel groaned because of the bondage, and they cried out; and their cry came up to God because of the bondage. So God heard their groaning, and God remembered His covenant with Abraham, with Isaac, and with Jacob. And God looked upon the children of Israel, and God acknowledged them" (Exod. 2:23–25).

All throughout the Scriptures you can see God establishing the principle of audibly calling out to Him for justice: "Call upon Me in the day of trouble; I will deliver you, and you shall glorify Me" (Ps. 50:15). The Hebrew word for "call" is *qara*, and it means "calling aloud or crying aloud." David the psalmist found it necessary to cry out continually: "Evening and morning and at noon I will pray, and cry aloud, and He shall hear my voice" (55:17). The Hebrew word here for "crying aloud" is *hamah*, which means "a loud roar." Other Hebrew words mentioned in the Bible that describe crying out to God are *shava*, a high-pitched shout for help, *tse'aqah*, a cry of distress, and *rinnah*, a ringing cry of grief or a joyful shout.

In the New Testament Paul also instructs us to cry out to God: "For you did not receive the spirit of bondage again to fear, but you received the Spirit of adoption by whom we cry out, 'Abba, Father'" (Rom. 8:15). The word Paul uses here for "cry" is *krazo*, and it literally means "to shout."

How Long Do You Have to Wait?

So, when will God's justice come your way? Two statements from the parable of the persistent widow give us the answer. The first clue is in Luke 18:7: "And shall God not avenge His own elect who cry out day and night to Him, though He bears long with them?" The word here for "bears long" is *makrothumeo*, and it means to patiently endure loss and misfortune. God is merciful toward you when you're suffering an injustice, so much so that He carries the burden of injustice with you, bearing you up under the heavy load you're carrying. *Makrothumeo!* In essence, God endures your pain with you and longs for the dawning day of your vindication even more than you do.

Why is it necessary that you bear this burden so long? Because, as we've discussed, God is concerned about not only what happens *to* you but also what happens *in* you. In this long season of suffering and loss, God is refining and molding you. There is a wonderful truth in James 5:7 that affirms this: "Therefore be patient, brethren, until the coming of the Lord. See how the farmer waits for the precious fruit of the earth, waiting patiently for it until it receives the early and latter rain." The early rain broke up the fallow and hard ground and prepared the soil for the seed. The latter rain germinated the seed, and the farmer waited patiently, bearing long, for the seed to take root. First the stalk, then the blade, then the full kernel of wheat.

Yes, the farmer longed for harvesttime but also knew it was necessary for the early and latter rains to complete their work. Your times and seasons are in the hands of a loving and just God who knows exactly when your soul is ready to receive the harvest of justice you've been crying out to obtain.

Our second clue concerning when our justice will come is found in Luke 18:8: "I tell you that He will avenge them speedily." After you cry out to God in patient endurance your justice is going to come, and when it does it will be quick and sure—speedily! The amazing Greek word here for "speedily" is *tachista*, from which we get our word *tachometer*. It carries the meaning of quickness, or a short amount of time. As you and God bear long through this season of injustice, rest assured that *Elohei Mishpat*, the God of Justice, is going to avenge you soon.

The Two Rs: Restoration and Restitution

God is so faithful to His name, *Elohei Mishpat*, that He not only brings restoration but also restitution. In restoration the God of

Justice returns what we have lost. In restitution the God of Justice compensates us for all the pain and suffering we have endured through our long season of loss. The Shunammite woman in 2 Kings is a wonderful example of this double deliverance. The prophet Elisha warned her of a coming famine in Israel, and so she moved to a foreign country for seven years. When she returned she found her house and land had been taken over by others. She appealed to the king for justice, "So the king appointed a certain officer for her, saying, 'Restore all that was hers'" (2 Kings 8:6). She got her land and home back. That's restoration! But there's a second half to verse 6: "and all the proceeds of the field from the day that she left the land until now." Others had unjustly confiscated her land in her absence and the king ordered them to pay her all the profits in full from the harvests of the seven years she was away. That's restitution!

If you have been a victim of someone else's abuse or fallen prey to the attack of the adversary, you are eligible for a settlement from the God of Justice that includes both a full restoration and compensation for lost time, emotional pain and suffering, lost inheritance, seasons of barrenness and fruitlessness due to spiritual drought, loss of finances, loss of a job or income due to an economic downturn, and even loss of joy and happiness. Your job is to make a claim. Isaiah tells us that in his day, "No one calls for justice" (Isa. 59:4). But you can change that in your day by taking a stand like the persistent widow in Luke 18 and cry out for your vindication. God is longing to vindicate His great name—*Elohei Mishpat*—and He's calling you to get involved in your own restoration and restitution by lifting up your voice in a cry for justice.

A Plant Built on a Decree

Now, for the rest of the story of the decree for justice for Mobile. It would have been hard to believe if I hadn't seen it with my own eyes.

After we cried out to God on the airfield that morning on May 10, 2010, we waited patiently and continued to ask God for justice on behalf of our city. What happened next has everything to do with God "bearing long" and carrying our burden with us.

As we waited, humility began to grow in the business leaders involved. They began to see that God's ultimate purpose for the city of Mobile was of kingdom value not just economic value. Hearts were knit together and our prayers became deeper and more significant. Yet in changing our mandate from economics to righteousness, we never let go of the burden to continue to cry out for justice.

Then suddenly, unexpectedly, and speedily, our justice came—two years after our loss—in a way that was beyond what we had asked or hoped; it was a full restoration and restitution moment. On July 2, 2012, Airbus held a press conference in downtown Mobile, and when the Airbus official got up to speak he stunned both the city and the worldwide aerospace community. He explained how Airbus now planned to build a $600 million assembly plant in Mobile, Alabama, in order to construct the A-320, a large 150-seat luxury airliner equivalent in size to a Boeing 737. Over the next few years the factory was constructed and the first A-320 rolled off the assembly line on March 21, 2016—appropriately, the first day of spring. Would you like to know where Airbus built their building? Right on top of our decree for justice! Not long after the stunning Airbus announcement we gathered again at dawn on the airfield to lift our voices in thanksgiving and praise to God for His remarkable mercy. Two of the godly men who were intricately involved in writing the decree for justice soon after ran for public office. Sandy Stimpson was elected mayor of Mobile, and Bill Hightower was elected state senator.

Our reasonable, necessary act: we cried out and we waited. Our Abba Father reached his hands down into Airbus and did more than we could ever have imagined.

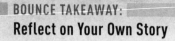

BOUNCE TAKEAWAY:
Reflect on Your Own Story

1. I said in this chapter that God is not only concerned about what happens to you but also what happens in you. What concerns might God presently have about things inside you? What do you think He might be trying to accomplish in you through this season of loss?

2. Has the knowledge that the very core of God's being is justice brought you assurance that your vindication is sure?

3. We talked in this chapter about the principle of crying out to God for justice. As you consider lifting your voice in a cry for justice, what are your hesitations? From what we studied, do you think the benefits of crying out outweigh any possible feelings of self-consciousness you might have?

BOUNCE CHALLENGE #12

In your bounce journal, I encourage you to write a decree for justice. Ask God for vindication, restoration, and restitution. You can open this entry with the heading "My Decree for Justice."

CONCLUSION

You, too, can bounce back! My prayer for you is that you will break through the roadblocks of self-pity, disappointment, resentment toward God, and indecisiveness. I pray you will liquidate some of the toxic mental real estate from your past story, embrace the perplexity of your loss, start hoping with the slaves of the West Indies, and cry out to God for justice. Your first day of spring, that bright day of your full restoration and restitution, is coming very soon, because God is *Elohei Mishpat*, the God of Justice. And He is good.

Until then, in the words of Matthew Lawson, "Press on regardless!"

FINAL BOUNCE TAKEAWAY

Romans 8:28 says that "all things work together for good to those who love God, to those who are the called according to His purpose." As you think about the painful things you are going through right now and look forward to them all working out for your good, the question is: How do you define "good"? Is "good" just getting your stuff back and your life back and experiencing vindication, restoration, and restitution for all the things you've lost in this downturn moment of your life? Or is "good" something even deeper? Could it be that after a season of loss and heartache "good" should actually be measured by how much closer you are to Jesus and how much of His character and nature have been imparted to you through your suffering? Think about this: What's the better good of coming back from loss—having your life back or having His life in you?

 FINAL BOUNCE CHALLENGE

Let's start a movement together! There are people in your sphere of influence who need to discover what you've experienced in our journey through *Bounce*, and you can help them get into our resilience movement. How? Simply find one person living in the depths of despair because of a painful loss and share with them what you've learned about bouncing back. Tell them your story of heartache and how the Lord is bringing you back from the brink. The only way you can make sense out of your pain is if it brings you closer to God and inspires in you empathy for others who are hurting.

ACKNOWLEDGMENTS

I debated whether or not to write acknowledgments this time around. "Keep it simple," I said. "No one reads the acknowledgments anyway," I said. "Minimalism is better," I said. But then I realized a book is a collection of thoughts, concepts, and sometimes pictures the writer forms from human experience—the people he has met along the road who had something to say from time to time, either through words or deeds or observation of their lives—that challenged and changed him, adding richness to his soul. So here are a few hymns of thanks to all those who have made this book a reality. The pages between these covers would be shy of ink should I have never crossed paths with them.

A hymn of praise to the women in my life:

Sharon—after all these years I still awake every morning wondering how I was able to capture your heart. You are my partner in resilience and I can't imagine living without you. *Atem maor einye*—you are the light of my eyes.

Rachel, Elizabeth, and Hannah—my daughters—you have all shown me how life is a celebration that gets sweeter over time. I am amazed by your *chutzpah*—that shameless audacity that finds a way when there is no way. Now that you all three have come into womanhood and I observe your unique and powerful leadership giftings, there are times I tremble in your presence.

Michelle McKinney Hammond—my daughter in the faith—you have taught me the value of a heart fully and completely submitted to God. You sat in the front row of our church for eight years with your Bible open, listening to my sermons. Today your gifts of teaching and writing have surpassed mine a million times over.

Kathy Watson—my big sister. You, my dear, are of noble character. Your life fills every page of this book and you have taught me to love through the pain. Thank you for reading through the manuscript, adding your editorial insights, encouraging me to write my—no, *our*—story, and once again cleaning up your little brother's messes before I sent it off to the publisher!

Teresa Evenson—my agent from the William Jensen Literary Agency—you have taught me that little things really matter and have helped me to sharpen my skills, lengthen my cords, and strengthen my stakes. You're the best!

A hymn of praise to the men in my life:

Nathan Früh—my son—you, boy, have taught me to never give up in life or on the tennis court. You have also reminded me that young boys can still become men before their time. I am proud of you, Nathan, for desiring the things God desires. I love you, son.

Matthew Cuccias and Stuart Wann—my sons-in-law—you both have taught me that God answers a man's prayers concerning the godly character of his daughters' future husbands.

Thank you for covering them with your masculine protection. I love you as my own.

Mike Gottfried—you have modeled to me tenacity in the face of overwhelming odds.

Mike Coleman—you have modeled to me quiet but bold leadership under extreme pressure.

Danny Sellers—you have modeled to me unhindered loyalty and dedication even when the way is not clear.

Stuart Roth—you have taught me the meaning of lifelong friendship.

Tom Arington—you have taught me that a life story should include not only the triumphs but the troubles. Your life story encourages me that I, too, can face difficult challenges while living in victory at the same time.

Lars Eric Svensson—my father-in-law—you have shown me a resilience that is almost otherworldly. At eighty-nine years of age you are still building churches, orphanages, and schools in the third world. Amazing!

A hymn of praise to my grandchildren:

Avery, Asher, and Ellie—just when I thought life was beginning to get boring, you three came along. You have taught *Zadie* (Yiddish for grandfather) that living a resilient life is so worth it, because life keeps coming around full circle if I just hold on, and now that you've arrived I get to hear the pitter-patter of little feet on my hardwood floors once again.

A hymn of praise to Baker Publishing Group: this is the third book you have published for me. You have taught me the value of relationship. Thank you for your integrity in ministry. Thank you to Rebekah Guzman, senior acquisitions editor at Baker, for believing in the concept of *Bounce*. And a huge thanks to Jamie

Chavez, my editor. You, my dear, have to be the best in the business! I must admit your first edit was worse than a root canal. Ouch! Your insights made *Bounce* so much stronger. Thank you for telling me the truth.

Finally, I want to give thanks to a person in my life who has been the greatest example of resilience: Joe Walvis, holocaust survivor, hemophiliac, handicapped person, and multimillionaire business leader. Joe had the uncanny ability to face severe perplexity with unbelievable joy and laughter. He taught me more about overcoming loss than anyone I have ever met. Joe is now with the Lord, and he never knew it but I loved him like a son loves a father. I just wish I would have told him so. The day he died, I wailed. I miss him terribly.

NOTES

Chapter 2 You Were Made to Bounce

1. *The Tigger Movie*, directed by Jun Falkenstein (Burbank, CA: Walt Disney Company, 2000).

2. Dr. Caroline Leaf, *Who Switched Off My Brain?* (Nashville: Thomas Nelson, 2009), 16, 99.

3. Ibid., 133–34.

Chapter 3 Reframe Your Loss

1. John Steinbeck, *Travels with Charley: In Search of America* (Westminster, London: Penguin Publishing Group, 2012), from the introduction.

2. C. S. Lewis, *The Problem of Pain* (New York: Macmillan, 1962), 93.

3. Viktor E. Frankl, *Man's Search for Meaning* (Boston: Beacon Press, 1959), 10.

Chapter 5 Self-Pity

1. *The Princess Bride*, directed by Rob Reiner (Burbank, CA: Twentieth Century-Fox, 1987).

Chapter 6 Disappointment

1. Eugene H. Peterson, ed., "Job: Led by Suffering to the Heart of God," *The Message* (Colorado Springs: Navpress, 1996).

2. Elie Wiesel, *Night* (New York: Hill and Wang, 1972, 1985), 4–5.

Chapter 7 Resentment toward God

1. Guy Walters, "The Wall of Love and Sorrow," *The Daily Mail*, December 23, 2013, http://www.dailymail.co.uk/news/article-2528664.

2. Brett Buckner, "Staring into the Void: God and the Holocaust," *The Aniston Star*, March 27, 2005, 29.

3. Arthur Katz, *The Holocaust: Where Was God?* (Laporte, MN: Burning Bush Publications, 1988), from the introduction.

4. Wiesel, *Night*, 64–65.

5. Charles Allen Dinsmore, *Atonement in Literature and Life* (London: Constable, 1906), 232.

6. Charles Wesley, "And Can It Be That I Should Gain," 1738.

7. Jonathan Jones, "Hidden Horror," *The Guardian*, December 12, 2007, https://www.theguardian.com/artanddesign/2007/dec/12/art?CMP=share_bt_.

8. Dennis Ngien, "The God Who Suffers," *Christianity Today*, February 3, 1997, http://www.christianitytoday.com/ct/1997/february3/7t2038.html.

9. Catherine Shoard, "Son of Saul Star: 'God Was Holding the Hand of Every Jew in the Gas Chamber,'" *The Guardian*, May 19, 2015, https://www.theguardian.com/film/2015/may/19/geza-rohrig-son-of-saul-interview-auschwitz-jewish-prisoner-sonderkommando?CMP=share_btn_link.

Chapter 8 Indecisiveness

1. *Braveheart*, directed by Mel Gibson (Hollywood, CA: Paramount Pictures, 1995).

2. Laura Hillenbrand, *Seabiscuit: An American Legend* (New York: Random House, 2001), 314.

3. Ibid., 349.

4. Ibid., 351.

Chapter 9 Liquidate Some Mental Real Estate

1. Pat Conroy, *Vanity Fair* 58, no. 7 (July 1995), 108.

Chapter 12 Cry Out for Justice

1. Aaron Früh, *The Decree of Esther* (Grand Rapids: Chosen, 2004), 158–59.

ABOUT THE AUTHOR

Aaron Früh is a pastor, national radio personality, regional television host, amateur house restorer, and an expert when it comes to loss. He experienced loss early on when his father was killed by a drunk driver when he was three years old. Growing up in a single-parent home, he learned the value of bouncing back from life's losses and struggles. Rather than being defeated by loss, he saw it as an admired mentor. His favorite quote is "Some days you win and other days you learn." Learning to depend on God for restitution and restoration, Aaron developed amazing recuperative powers, a deep well of love and compassion, and a great sense of humor. He has been forged in the fire of loss and made stronger and more resilient, which has become his life message and one he is passionate about sharing.

Aaron is the vice president of education and development for Israel Team Advocates International, a nonprofit organization that mentors athletes, coaches, and business leaders, helping them gain a deeper understanding about the Jewish people and the nation of Israel. Aaron was the lead pastor of Knollwood Church in Mobile, Alabama, for twenty-four years. He is a graduate of Bethany University (BS in Theology) and Wheaton College Graduate School

(MA in Christian Education). From 2009–2011 Aaron was also a featured guest speaker at the monthly Promise Keepers national conventions. During these years these monthly PK events had attendance ranging from five to fifteen thousand.

Aaron is a weekly guest on the nationally syndicated radio program *Nothing but Truth* with Crane Durham, which airs on the American Family Radio network. His thirty-minute segment, *Afternoons with Aaron*, covers a wide range of issues concerning Christian growth and Israel. It is broadcast on AFR's two hundred stations, reaching an audience of over four million people. Aaron has been a part of this program for the past five years. The American Family Association has also featured him on several one-hour special simulcasts. Aaron recently launched a new website, www.aaronfruh.com.

Aaron has been married to Dr. Sharon Früh for thirty-five years. They have four children and three grandchildren and reside in Point Clear, Alabama.